Copyright 2022 by Thobekile Creddy Siziba

All rights reserved. No part of this book may be reproduced or used in any manner without the written permission of the owner of the copyright except for the use in quotations in a book review.

ISBN: 9798846371071

Independently published

NAMBITHA IZIBILIBOCO

A Selection of Zimbabwean Traditional Recipes

Junior Edition

Thobekile Creddy Siziba

OKUMAYELANA LOMLOBI

Umlobi u Thobekile Creddy Siziba wazalelwa esigabeni sase Setshele emangweni we-Insiza ngo 1951. Uyise engu Sibangwa ethethe omaDube. Isikolo ukufunda uqalele koSikhobo eTsholotsho ehlala kwabomkhulu koMpango Dube. Wayake funda leSaziyabana, eGwelutshena eGampinya leTsheli. Imfundo engaphezulu waba seMatopo Mission ngo 1969 - 1972. Wafundela ke ubutitsha eGwanda. E UK ubese University of East London (2003-2004) esenza i Third World Development with NGOs Management (International Sudies) ihlangene leEducation and Community Studies. Wabase Matthew Bolton leJoseph Chamberlain colleges esenzi International Citizenship. E Focus khona wenza iFitness Instructor ayevele ekewaku fundela eBulawayo Studios leMuscle and Caves ngasikhathi sinye leSwimming ayeyenziswa ngu Superintendent Cephas Mpofu Soganile kuBarrow loMnu Moyo eLuveve nxa kuyimpela Viki 1993-1994. Ufundisile eNgwaladi, Butabubili, Mhlabangubo, Saziyabana, Mzilikazi, Sigombe le Fusi. E UK wafundisa kafitshane e Orpington Threshers Day Care le eRedhouse primary school ngaphansi kwe Walsall engakaqhatshwa okupheleleyo. Ubese Botswana ngama early 70's lango 1999-2001. Use UK lentombi zakwakhe oNothando, Nomagugu loNokuthula Zanele labazukulu. Ijaha uNqobizitha leyakhimuli beseZimbabwe. UCreddy ubekuthanda ukupheka njengayo yonke imisebenzi yangekhaya, loba esakhula. Ubekhuthazwa ngabazali, ogogo, odadewabo, oyisekazi kanye lababalisi bezokupheka. Ethanda njalo ezemidlalo, ukuthunga, ukuhlabela lokweluka iwulu. Ulobe ezinye inkondlo ekuqembu le Writers Without Borders. Okwamanje ukwele Pens Erdington. Ubambene njalo labanye abathathu ku Once Upon A Child.

ABOUT THE AUTHOR

The author Thobekile Creddy Siziba was born at the village of Setshele in the Insiza District in 1951. Her parents were Sibangwa and maDube. She started school at Sikhobo St Barbara school in Tsholotsho living with her marternal grandparents Mpango Dube and maSibanda. She then went to continue in Nkayi at Saziyabana, Gwelutshena, Gampinya and Tsheli. Her higher education was at Matopo Mission 1969-72. She did teacher training at Gwanda. In the UK she went to the University of East London 2003- 2004 doing, Third World Development with NGOs Management (International Studies) combined with Education and Community Studies. At Matthew Bolton and Joseph Chamberlain colleges she did International Citizenship and with Focus, she did the fitness instructors course which she had previously done at Bulawayo Studios and Muscle and Curves, at the same time with the swimming course coached by superintendent Cephas Mpofu Soganile at Barrow and Moyo at Luveve during the weekends, 1993-94. She taught at Ingwaladi, Butabubili, Mhlabangubo, Mzilikazi, Sigombe and Fusi. In the UK she briefly taught voluntarily at Threshers in Orpington and at Redhouse primary school in Aldridge under Walsall. She was in Botswana in the early 70's and then in 1999 to 2001. In the UK she is here with all her three daughters Nothando, Nomagugu and Nokuthula Zanele. Her only son Nqobizitha Mpofu and his family are still in Zimbabwe. Creddy used to like cooking from a young age, like all other domestic chores. She benefited from her inspirational parents, grandmothers, aunts, sisters and Domestic Science teachers. She also loves sports, sewing, music and knitting. She wrote poems for a while with Writers Without Borders and now with Pens of Erdington, both in Birmingham. She has appeared with 3 other friends for Once Upon A Child.

ULUHLU LWEZIHLOKO

Topic		Page
	Okuphekwayo	1
1	Amatshakada kumbe umngqutshu	3
2	Umxhanxa	7
3	Ilambazi	11
4	Umumbu omanzi	17
5	Inopi kumbe Isijeza	23
6	Amagwadla	25
7	Isitshwala	29
8	Amahewu	33
9	Amaqebelengwane	37
10	Inkobe	39
11	Amakhowa	45
12	Idobi	51
13	Amacimbi	55
14	Amathanga lamakhomane	59
15	Isahlaka Isathubi le Sathiyane	63
16	Umcaba	69
17	Idelele	75
18	Ufutho	79
19	Imbhida	81
20	Utshwala	89
	Izimpendulo	99

TABLE OF CONTENTS

Topic		Page
	What is cooked and where	2
1	Samp - skinless/coat-less maize	4
2	Mixture of melon and dry maize kernels	8
3	Porridge	12
4	Fresh Soft maize/corn	18
5	Mixture of melon and maize meal to thick porridge	24
6	Cooked/boiled dry maize kernels	26
7	Maize meal, sorghum or millet flour thick porridge	30
8	Maize meal, sorghum or millet drink	34
9	Dumpling like balls kneaded and rolled with maize meal, sorghum or millet flour dough	38
10	Mixture of peanuts, peas, beans or groundnuts/roundnuts with dry maize kernels	40
11	Mushrooms	46
12	Peanut butter	52
13	Edible caterpillars/Maphane worms	56
14	Pumpkins and tender gourds	60
15	Milk dishes of colostrum and whole milk	64
16	Mixture of Curds and cooked then ground sorghum or millet	70
17	Okra	76
18	Boiled and dried soft maize kernels recooked	80
19	Green leafy Vegetables fresh or dried	82
20	Traditional beer	90
	Answers	100

OKUPHEKWAYO

Emkulwini kusekhitshini Phela njalo yikho lapho esiphekela khona ukudla siphinde sikwejise khona. Omama labogogo obabakazi, amantombazana, labantwana yibo endulo abebetholakala kakhulu besemkulwini. Bebeyabe bepheka njalo bexoxa befundisana okunengi. Obaba labokhulu belamajaha labafana ezibayeni ledale befundisana okwabo labo bekhukhuza awabo amathambo phela.

OMAMA ABAGIGAYO

Fun Activity:

Ngamunye ngababili kumbe ngabathathu, lingiselanini abagigayo.

Q: Qamba izinto ezimbili ezingagigwa.

Q: Ekugigeni kusetshenziswani?

WHAT IS COOKED AND WHERE

In the kitchen "*emkulwini*" is where we cook food and we spend most of our free time there. Mothers, grandmothers, aunts, girls and children are the ones in yesteryear you would find in the kitchen. They would be discussing and teaching each other various things. Fathers and grandfathers would be with younger men and boys by the kraals, cowsheds or special "*indaba*" encircled areas "*edale*" teaching each other important manhood topics, 'chewing their own bones', "*bekhukhuza awabo amathambo*".

MOTHERS POUNDING

Fun Activity:

As individuals or in pairs or threes, imitate or pretend to be pounding mothers or girls.

Q: Name two things that can be pounded.

Q: Discuss what is used when pounding.

01 AMATSHAKADA KUMBE UMNQUTSHU

- Thatha umumbu uwugige engigeni ngomgigo.
- Lokhu yikuwu khipha isikuba hatshi ukuwenza impuphu.
- Ukhiphele esitsheni ubusuwu phephetha ngokhomane ukhipha phela isikuba lesi esihlubekileyo.
- Ugezise ngamanzi aqandayo ubusuwuthela embizeni evele isilamanzi akhudumalayo eziko. Amanzi abengaphezudlwana komumbu.
- Sibekela ke imbiza ngesidekiselo.
- Yekela kuxhwathe emlilweni olingeneyo ukuze kungatsheli.
- Nxa amanzi esemalutshwana isixhwathela phansi, thela njalo amanzi akhudumalayo ufake isawudo elilingeneyo elizazwela.
- Ungalokothi uthele amanzi aqandayo ngoba ayagwanyisa okuphekwayo kungazabe kusavuthwa kuhle.
- Kungavuthwa, yephuli mbiza uphakulule nxa kuzadliwa kunjalo kukodwa kumbe kusiba ngumgqutshu kudliwa lenyama.
- Kungadliwa njalo lochago oluluhlaza.

01 SAMP

- Samp is what is left after skins have been removed from maize kernels, or corn during which process the maize cracks or breaks into pieces.
- Take maize kernels and pound them in the wooden pounding vessel "*ingiga*" with the pounding log "*umgigo*".
- This is the process for removing maize skins but not pounding it into powder, mealie meal or maize flour like "*iwisa*".
- Remove it into an "*isitsha*" or a clean dry dish or bowl and winnow it to remove the skin, chaff and husks with "*ukhomane*"
- Wash the Samp with cold water and pour it into a pot that should already be on the stove or fire with hot or boiling water. The water should cover the Samp.
- Cover the pot or saucepan with a lid.
- Let it cook, simmering on a low heat.
- When the water gets too low, add more warm water. Add enough salt depending on amount of food and your taste.
- Never pour on cold water because it causes the food to harden and not cook properly.
- When it is well cooked, take the pot and dish the Samp out.

01 AMATSHAKADA KUMBE UMNGQUTSHU

- Kwesinye isikhathi kuyabondelwa idobi embizeni nxasekuvuthiwe. Ulaza olwengulwa echagweni oseluvuthiwe lalo lungathelwa embizeni nxa ukudla sekuvuthiwe kuphenduphendulwe kuhlangane kuhle. Amatshakada angaphekwa njalo ehlanganiswe lendumba.
- indlubu kumbe amazambane. Hawu uyangcinda unathe laloba yikuphi okuthandayo.
- usehlisa ulale ngabe utshone ngesikhulu.

Phendula Le Imibuzo

Q: Uthela amanzi anjani uma imbiza isisitsha ingakavuthwa?

Q: Kuyini okuthathu esingaku hlanganisa lamatshakada?

Q: Abizwa kuthiweni amatshakada adliwa lenyama njengawo mtshado?

01 SAMP *Continued*

- When eaten with meat, it is called "umgqutshu". It can also be eaten with warm fresh milk.

- Sometimes peanut butter "idobi" is added to Samp while it is still cooking but when it is well cooked. Cream can also be added to Samp while in the cooking pot. These become different and delicious varieties of the dish.

- One can also cook Samp with dry cowpeas "indumba", roundnuts "indlubu" or with peanuts "amazambane". These are other types of a vital traditional dish that you can enjoy with any type of drink you prefer as an accompaniment.

Answer These Questions

Q: What kind of water should you pour on or add into the cooking pot?

Q: What other three ingredients can be cooked or mixed with Samp?

Q: What do we call Samp eaten with some meat?

02 UMXHANXA

- Khetha ijodo olifunayo uma emanengi.
- Thatha ingqamu usikelele ijodo lakho endaweni ehlanzekileyo.
- Khipha intanga loqweqwe amakokobi phela encezwini ozisikelelayo.
- Ungasikelelela enditshini yemiganu ehlanzekileyo.
- Thela incezu embizeni eseziko elamanzi angaba ngaphezudlwana nje kocezu lokuqala.
- Yekela kuxhwathe kuzekuvuthwe unanzelele imbiza ingalulumeli eziko icitshe umlilo.
- Kungavuthwa phehla ngophehlo uthele amagwadla akho avele lawo esevuthiwe uqhubeke uphehla ukuze kuhlangane kuhle.
- Usunga phakululela emiganwini ezingubhe kudliwe.
- Abanye bathanda kuletshukela.
- Umxhanxa ungaphekwa njalo ngejodo elasikelelwa lachaywa loma labangumpale unkankalo phela.
- Unkankalo luyasikelelwa luthelwe embizeni eseziko elamanzi amalutshwana.
- Sibekela wekele kuxhwathe ube uphendula ngemva kwesikhathi esithile kuzekuvuthwe.
- Phehla ke njengalokhu okwenze ijodo elimanzi ngaphezulu. Thela amagwadla akho avele esevuthiwe uqhubeke uphehla kuhlangane.
- Yephula uphakulule kuphole mbijana kudliwe ngezikhezo izipunu phela.
- Umnandi umxhanxa njalo uyasuthisa uyaqinisa umzimba ugezise lezinso.

02 MELON WITH DRY MAIZE KERNELS

- Choose a good melon if you have many to choose from.
- Using a sharp knife, cut the melon into pieces lengthwise. Remove the seeds and peel the outside.
- You then cut it into smaller pieces putting them in a clean dish or bowl.
- Put the pieces into a pot with hot water on the stove or fireplace. Let the water be slightly above your melon pieces. Leave to cook until soft, making sure that it does not boil over.
- When satisfactorily cooked, smooth with the wooden mixer called an "uphehlo" or any other type beater you have available.
- Now you can add the already cooked dry maize kernels "amagwadla" and mix well.
- You can now dish out the food into bowls. Eat with wooden, metal or any other type of spoon. Some people like "umxhanxa" with sugar.
- Instead of using fresh melons, you can also use the dried ones preserved for off-season time called "unkankalo/umpale".
- Similarly, you cut the dry melon pieces into even smaller pieces. Put these into a pot with boiling or hot water. Cover and leave to simmer, stirring at intervals of about 8 minutes until cooked soft and tender.
- Stir with the beater "uphehlo" until smooth just as you do with the fresh melon.
- Pour in the already cooked dry maize kernels, "amagwadla" and continue mixing.
- Take the pot off the heat, let the food cool a little before serving.
- Let people eat it with any type of spoon "izipunu/izikhezo". You can add sugar if you like.
- This traditional dish is nice and filling "kuyasuthisa" plus, due to its water content, it helps digestion "ukugaywa kokudla esiswini", the bladder "isinye" and kidneys "izinso".

02 UMXHANXA

Phendula Le Imibuzo

Q: *Kuyini okuhlanganiswa ekuphekeni umxhanxa?*

Q: *Sihlanyelani ukuze intanga ihlanze ijodo?*

Q: *Kuyini unkankalo?*

02 MELON WITH DRY MAIZE Continued

Answer These Questions

Q: What is mixed when cooking this "umxhanxa" dish? Discuss.

Q: What do we sow in the fields or garden in order to get melons?

Q: What is "unkankalo(u)"?

03　ILAMBAZI

- Ilambazi limele liphekwe ngobungcitshi lobunono njengakho konke okunye ukudla kweSintu.
- Liyikudla kwekuseni okwenza usuku luqalele phezulu kakhulu.
- Liphekwa ngempuphu yomumbu, eyophoko kumbe eyamabele.
- Thela impuphu esiphathelweni esiyingubhe ubunengi bube mayelana lobukhulu bembiza esetshenziswayo kunye lenani labantu abaphekelwayo.
- Thela amanzi aqandayo emputshini uvubanise kuhlangane kuhle.
- Thelake embizeni ngonanzelelo.
- Imbiza ibingevele isilamanzi atshisayo eziko, ugoqozele ngophini sonke isikhathi ukuze kungabundeli kwenze amabhundu.
- Thela amanye amanzi atshisayo nxa kujiya kakhulu uqhubeke ugoqoza kumbe uphehla ngophehlo kuphele wonke amapundl.
- Nxa ilambazi selixhwatha kuhle, lingalulumi, mbokotha ngesib uyekele kuxhwathe imizuzu engaba litshumi lanhlanu.
- Phendula ilambazi ubusufaka itshukela kumbe ledobi, ibhata, isawujwanyana kumbe ilemoni okweneleyo.

03 PORRIDGE

- Porridge has to be cooked skilfully, like any other traditional food.
- It is food eaten in the morning as breakfast hence it helps one start the day on a high note. It is mainly cooked with maize meal "*impuphu yomumbu*", finger millet "*eyophoko*", or sorghum flour "*impuphu yamabele*".
- Pour *mealie* meal into a bowl enough for the number of people and the pot size.
- Add cold water and mixer well into a paste.
- Carefully pour into the pot or saucepan on the stove or fire with water that is already boiling.
- Keep stirring to prevent it going lumpy.
- If it is getting too thick, pour on a little boiling water and continue stirring.
- If it is smooth and simmers nicely, cover the pot with a lid "*sibekelo/ isidekiselo*".
- Let it cook for about 10 minutes.
- Open the pot and stir again adding enough sugar as well as either peanut butter "*idobi*", butter "*ibhata*", salt "*isawudo*" or lemon "*ilemoni*" to your own taste.

03 ILAMBAZI

- Yekela kuxhwathaxhwathe okwemizuzu engaba litshumi kusiya ngobukhulu bembiza.
- Yephula imbiza uphakululele emiganwini efaneleyo ukudla kungagelezeli phansi.
- Dlanini ngenkezo zokudla likholise.
- Abanye ke kwesinye isikhathi nxa sekusele ilambazi elilutshwana emiganwini, bayafaka intolwane baqediseke ukudla. Lokhu abadala bathi kuqinisa umzimba.
- Abanye bathanda ukudla ilambazi lilochago oluluhlaza.

03 PORRIDGE Continued

- Leave the porridge to simmer "ukuxhwatha" for about 10 more minutes "imizuzu elitshumi" depending on the size of the pot.
- Take the pot off the heat "yephula imbiza" and serve out "uphakulule" into bowls "imganu" although thick, not on flat plates "incence", as the food will spill "ukugelezela phansi/ukuchitheka".
- Serve and eat with spoons "izikhezo/izipunu".
- Sometimes, when there is a little porridge left in the plate, some people will add a traditional concoction called "Intolwane" and then finish it off. This, elders say, is a medicine for tightening and strengthening the body especially the joints. You feel the tightening, even on your tongue.
- Some people like eating porridge with fresh milk too.

03 ILAMBAZI ELIBILISIWEYO

- Ilambazi lingaphekwa njalo ngempuphu ebilisiweyo.
- Hlanganisa impuphu lamanzi esiphathelweni kusale kuyinhlama ejiyileyo.
- Vala ke uyekele kulale kunjalo okobusuku bunye kumbe insuku ezimbili.
- Nxa sekubilile, thela embizeni elamanzi atshisayo eseziko ugoqozele njengesikwenze inhlanganiso yempuphu ngaphezulu.
- Pheka ngendlela efananayo kodwa ungahlanganisi lento enjenge lemoni ebabayo ngoba lelilambazi livele liphekwe ngenhlama ebabayo ebilileyo.
- Yephula imbiza uphakulule kudliwe.

Phendula Le Imibuzo

Q1: (a) Ilambazi lidliwa e_____.

(b) Liphekwa njalo kusongiwa og_____ , ob_____ kumbe os_____.

(c) Liphiwa njalo izi_____.

Q: Ilambazi eliphiwa izingane sithi yi_____.

Q: Ilambazi elimunyu sithi ngeli b_____.

03 PORRIDGE Continued - SOUR PORRIDGE

- Porridge can also be cooked using fermented mealie meal, grain flour.
- Put any grain flour you like into a bowl and mix well with cold water. Make the mixture "inhlama", smooth and not too thick.
- Cover the bowl and leave it overnight or better still, two days to ferment.
- When fermented, pour the mixture into a pot that already has hot or boiling water. Stir continuously as described before for the usual type of porridge.
- Use the same method to finish it except, do not add lemon or salt for this dish because it is already sour, just add enough sugar for your taste.
- Serve out and let the people eat and enjoy "yekela abantu badle bakholise".

Answer These Questions

Q: At what time of the day is porridge eaten _____?

Discuss that it is also prepared when looking after a person, when it is called what _____? or given to a person that has _____?
It is also fed to _____?

Q: The porridge given to babies is called _____.

Q: Sour porridge is said to be _____?

04 UMUMBU OMANZI

- Umumbu omanzi udliwa uphekiwe, wosiwe kumbe ucholiwe ukuwufahla phela uwubumbabumbe ubeyizinkwa zomfahlwa.
- Izinkwa lezi zifuna umumbu osese ngamachaphazi olula ukuchola lokubumbeka.
- Izinkwa zomfahlwa ziphekwa zigoqelwe ngamakhasi ahlutshwe kiwo umumbu 10 ophekwayo owosiwayo kumbe ohululwe wacholwa. Zifakwa letshukela nxa uthanda.
- Geca umumbu ovuthiweyo uwuhlube usale ulamakhasi amalutshwane nxa ungophekwayo.
- Faka umumbu embizeni elamanzi amanenganyana acwilisa umumbu osekuqaliseni.
- Mbokotha imbiza kuxhwathe kuzekuvuthwe.
- Yephula imbiza uphakulule.
- Abantu bayazihlubela badle.
- Abanye bathanda ukuwufaka isawudwanyana umumbu ophekiweyo.

04 SOFT MAIZE - ROAST OR GRILLED

- Soft maize/corn is traditionally "*ngesintu*", eaten either boiled, roasted or grilled "*wosiwe*" on the cob on wood fire embers. It is sometimes ground "*ukuwuchola*" or pounded "*ugigiwe*" then rolled and moulded into any desired shape or size, like buns, scones or dumplings, wrapped in its own husks and then cooked.
- Add sugar to taste.
- Put into the pot with hot water already there that covers the top layer.
- In the fields, choose and cut down the best soft maize plant. Cook the maize on the cob either with a few husks left on or without any.
- Remove all the corn-hair or corn-silk from the cob and kernels.
- Shell the kernels from the cob and pound or grind them to become "*umfahlwa*" if you are making "*izinkwa zomfahlwa*" bread loaves, tortillas or rolls made of "*umfahlwa*".
- Whichever of these methods you choose, put the amount of water "*amanzi*" that covers, "*acwilisa*", the first layer.
- Cover the pot and leave to cook, which could be about 30 minutes. If you check and they are not well cooked, add a little more hot water and leave longer.
- Remove from the fire or stove and dish out "*uphakulule*".
- You may leave the husks wrappings on for people to remove for themselves as they eat.
- Some people like to add a little salt "*isawudo*" to cooked corn or maize to suit your taste.

04 UMUMBU OMANZI

- Umumbu owosiwayo wona wande ukuhlutshwa wonke amakhasi wosiweke emalahleni esethe khehlelele.
- Wobuwu phenduphendula ukuze ungatshi.
- Nanzelela ungagiqagiqi umumbu emlotheni olenhlabathi kumbe enhlabathini ucine ungasadleki sulumela.
- Kawuvuthwe kuhle ubukeke umumbu ungahanguleki elangabini ubabe njalo unuke intuthu.
- Kayisibunandi bokudla umumbu owosiwayo ngabe ophekiweyo uhlanganisa lamazambane akhanzingiweyo odengezini loba aphekiweyo.

04 SOFT MAIZE Continued

- Roast maize "*umumbu owosiwayo*", as above, usually has all the husks and corn-silk removed from the cob and kernels before being roasted on red hot clean embers.
- Keep turning the cobs to prevent burning.
- Be careful "*unanzelele*" not to touch them with any sand or ashes if you are roasting on an open fire, this could damage your teeth as you chew.
- Let it cook well and get crispy but not be on fire because it would then cook prematurely and taste unpleasant, plus it will smell of smoke; this look would be neither attractive or appetising.
- No traditional dish tastes nicer than soft maize, boiled or roasted and then mixed with roast or grilled peanuts "*amazambane akhanzingiweyo*", or boiled ones, fresh or dried ones cooked with a bit of salt. What a tasty snack!

04 UMUMBU OMANZI

♦ Kulento ezondwa ngabantwana kodwa ethandwa ngabadala beyenza samdlalo. Lokhu kuthiwa yikuqalela umtwana indlela.

♦ Omdala uyamupha umtwana umumbu kodwa abasewuthatha ahulule umzila owodwa kumbe embili emithathu adle umtwana engakadli.

Phendula Le Imibuzo

Q: Umumbu ongama genyenga ongakaqinisisi sithi ungama _____.

Q: Umumbu okhahlelayo uphuma u _____.

Q: Umumbu omanzi singawudla u _____, u _____ kumbe uyizinkwa u _____.

Asizi thokozise

Hlabela ingoma yokusoma eyokuqalela umtwana indlela.

INGOMA le ngubani oyaziyo

UMtwana mtwana udobhu fudu lwakhe
Letha lapha ngimkwamulele
Hayi hayi uzamdlela
Hayi hayi angimdleli.
Yingoma ehlatshelwa kulingiswa kulandelwa inyoni enkulu emnyama emafusini kumbe egangeni. Ibizo lalinyoni kuthiwa yinsingizi.
Abanye bayayihlabela beqalela umtwana indlela ngokuhulula badle umumbu wakhe.

04 SOFT MAIZE Continued

- There is something that children do not like but some adults will laugh and make it into a game. It is called starting "*ukuqala/ukuqalela*", the path "*indlela*", the way or journey for the child, "*umtwana*" or "*ukuqalela umtwana indlela*".

- The older person gives the child a cob of maize roasted or boiled, but "*kodwa*" then ask for it back, shell off a line or two or even three lines and eat it before the child eats, so, before the 'owner' does. They say they are helping the child find the way. The child knows it's not quite necessary but, that is the sour joke.

Answer These Questions

Q: Very soft maize is called _____?

Q: As the maize plant matures, what comes out at the top _____?

Q: We can eat soft maize _____ or _____ or as a bun and is called _____?

Fun Activity

Sing the song for starting the pathway for a child.

Who knows that song?

The child "umtwana" has picked "udobhe" his or her tortoise "ufudu lwakhe".
Bring it here let me open and cut it for her/him "Letha lapha ngimkwamulele".
No no you will eat it for her "hayi hayi uzamdlela".
No no I will not eat it "hayi hayi" or "hatshi hatshi angimdleli".

This, originally, is a song sung when people imitate the sound made by the big black bird called the hornbill "*insingizi emnyama*". These birds are usually seen during the rainy season in the fields and plains hunting for locusts and other insects. This is the song that some people sing as they shell off children's corn kernels saying that they are starting the path for them.

05 INOPI KUMBE ISIJEZA

- Inopi iphekwa njengomxhangxa ngejodo elimanzi kumbe elonyisiweyo unkankalo njengoba sixoxe ngakho ngaphezulu.
- Umahluko ubakhona ekuthini kasihlanganisi lamagwadla kodwa sihlanganisa lempuphu.
- Nxa ijodo selivuthiwe uthela impuphu kangcane kancane ubonde kungabi lamapundu utshiye kulibundubundu elijiye mbijana kulelambazi.
- Faka itshukela eyeneleyo.
- Nxa ufuna ungafaka idobi ubonde ubususibekela uyekele imizuzwana engaba litshumi emlilweni olingeneyo ukuze kungatsheli.
- Yephuli mbiza eziko uphakulule kudliwe.
- Abanye bayithanda ilochago bezithelela emiganwini yabo.

Phendula Le Imibuzo

Q: Ijodo lizalwa kumbe lihlanzwa yini?

Q: Sithi kuyini ijodo eliwonyisiweyo?

Q: Qamba okubili okoku pheka inopi.

05 A MELON AND MEALIE MEAL / GRAIN FLOUR MIXTURE DISH

- "Inopi" is cooked like "umxhanxa" using a melon fresh or dried as we discussed before.
- The difference is that we do not use dry and then cooked maize "amagwadla". Instead, we mix melon with maize meal "impuphu yomumbu" or any other grain flour like millet or sorghum.
- When the melon is well cooked, beat and smooth it with a beater "uphehlo" and add mealie meal slowly, bit by bit. Stir with a stirring stick as it gets thicker to prevent going lumpy.
- Continue the process until it is thicker than porridge "ilambazi" but not too thick.
- Add enough sugar to taste, not too much sugar though, it depends on the size of your pot and amount of "inopi" in it.
- If you want you can add peanut butter "idobi" and stir well. Cover the pot with a lid and let it cook on a low heat for some minutes "imizuzu", about 10 "elitshumi". Make sure the food does not burn on the bottom.
- Stir and remove the pot from the fire or stove. Serve in dishes and let the family or visitors enjoy.
- Some like to eat "inopi" with fresh milk by just poring into their plates and mixing together.

Answer These Questions

Q: What do we call the vine that bears the melon?

Q: What do we call the cut and dried melons? Discuss.

Q: Name two ingredients we use to prepare or cook "inopi".

06 AMAGWADLA

- Cupha umumbu uwuphephethe ngokhomane ukhethe ukhiphe yonke ingcekeza.
- Thela lumumbu embizeni eseziko elamanzi azakuba ngaphezu komumbu owuthelayo.
- Yekela kuxhwathe kuzekuvuthwe ube uthela amanye amanzi akhudumalayo nxa isihuba sakutsha imbiza.
- Ungabona umumbu usuqala ukudabuka, asevuthiwe amagwadla akho.
- Abanye bathanda ukufaka isawudo.
- Usungafakake isawudo uyekele eziko imizuzu engaba mihlanu.
- Usungephula imbiza uphakulule kudliwe.
- Amagwadla amnandi njalo ekhanzingwe ndawonye lamazambane acacadiweyo.
- Nxa sekunje sikubiza sithi ngamaputi.
- Asibunandi balumqhina.
- Xoxanini ngomqhina lifunde okunye khonapho lisidla amaputi.

06 SHELLED MAIZE KERNELS

- Take enough grain for the size of pot you are using. Remove chaff by using a winnower "*ukhomane*" made of "*ilala*" plant fibres and broom grass "*umadodlwane*".
- Put the kernels into a pot with hot or boiling water. Have the water cover the ingredients.
- Cover and let it simmer until a few kernels start to pop or break open.
- If you find that the food is not yet well cooked, but the water is too low, pour extra hot or boiling water into the pot.
- Some people like to put salt "*isawudo*". You can leave to cook for five more minutes after putting in salt.
- Remove from the heat and serve.
- This dish is even nicer when you mix this "*amagwadla*" with roast peanuts.
- When mixed like that we then call it "*amaputi*". It is the Zimbabwean traditional 'popcorn' snack, very delicious.
- Discuss about "*umqhina*" while you are digging in and enjoying "*maputi*".

06 AMAGWADLA

- Ngensuku zayizolo amagwadla abesiba ngumphako omkhulu.
- Belingathwala umphako wenu lisiyakwelusa inkomo emadlelweni, lisiya esigayweni, lisiyasika utshani, lisiyagola amacimbi, lisiya siphuna imizi, ibhuma kumbe ingqodi, loba abafana besiyagamuli nyosi ukuyagebha izadenda amaminyela lengongomtshane kumbe besiyazingela. Kunathwe amanzi nje izisu zibengomatutlelana ilanga litshone bengananzelele abantu.

Phendula Le Imibuzo

Q: Amagwadla akhanzingwe lamazambane sithi ngama _____?

Q: Nxa sihamba uhambo olude amagwandla esihamba lawo sithi ngu _____?

Q: Aphekwa ngomumbu onjani amagwandla _____?

06 BOILED MAIZE KERNELS Continued

- In the past, "*amagwadla*" were eaten a lot when people were travelling long distances as "*umphako*" snacks.

- You could also carry it as a snack when going to herd cattle in the pastures "*emadlelweni*", going to the grinding mill "*esigayweni*" or going to fell trees "*ukuyagamula*". It was also carried by women going grass cutting "*ukuyasika utshani*", going to fetch amaphane worms, "*ukuyagola amacimbi*" or to fetch weaving grass "*imizi*" or "*inqodi*" for mats and "*izithebe*" or to fetch "*uswenyane, umnyankomo, ilala*" or "*umadodlwana*" for making traditional vessels like "*izitsha, ukhomane, izilulu, ingcebethu and izihluzo*". Men like to carry this type of snack when going to the forest to find honey "*inyosi*" or going to dig edible bulbs and root tubers like "*izadenda, izadloli*" or "*amaminyela*" roots as well as when they go hunting, "*ukuyazingela*".
They often drink water and feel so filled that they forget time is moving on for the tasks.

Answer These Questions

Q: Amagwadla boiled as they are or roasted when mixed with roast peanuts are called what _____?

Q: When we are travelling a long journey, what do we call "amagwadla" or the food that we carry_____?

Q: What kind of maize do we use as the main ingredient for this dish_____?

07 ISITSHWALA

- Beka imbiza eziko uthele amanzi ayisilinganiso osifunayo.
- Nxa amanzi esebila, cupha imputshana engcebethwini uyithele impuphu kancane kancane uphehla ngophehlo ukuze kungabi lamaqhubu phela.
- Ibundubundu lakho kumele lingajiyi kakhulu lale ukuxhwatha njalo lingabi lula kakhulu lilulume.
- Sibekelela imbiza uyekele ixhwathe okungaba yimizuzu elitshumi lanhlanu kusiya ngobukhulu be mbiza oyisebenzisayo.
- Nxa sekuxhwathe kwenela, sibukulula imbiza uphendule uthele impuphu kancane kancane ubonde ngophini.
- Bonda kuhlangane okuzwayo.
- Nxa isitshwala sesijiyé okweneleyo, sibekelela imbiza kumbe itswinye okungaba litshumi lemizuzu.
- Sibukulula imbiza ubonde uphendula uhlanganisa okuzwayo.
- Ungasibekela njalo uyekele okwemizuzu emine kumbe emihlanu.
- Phendula kuhlangane futhi ubususephula imbiza uphakululele isitshwala emiganwini kudliwe.

07 THICK PORRIDGE

- Put your pot on the fire or stove and pour enough water depending on the size of the pot or the number of people to be served. Leave the water to boil.
- When it is boiling, add maize meal slowly, or any other grain flour you decide to use, like sorghum or millet. Keep smoothing with a beater, "*ukuphehla*", or with the traditional beating stick "*uphehlo*" which you use by rolling it between both hands back and forth.
- The other method is to boil water in a kettle. Put enough flour, a cup full or half in a saucepan. Pour in cold water first and mix with the wooden flat stirring stick "*uphini*" before adding the hot water and then putting the pot on the fire. This is called "*ukugoqozela*".
- Continue stirring to prevent it going lumpy "*ukubundila*" or "*ukuba lamabhundu/amaqhubu*" lumps forming as you add in the boiling water from the kettle.
- Make sure that the mixture is not too thick, nor too watery.
- Cover the pot and let the porridge cook for about 10-15 minutes. This depends on the size of the pot and how much is being cooked.
- When it has cooked enough, add more of the flour bit by bit and mix well "*ukubonda*" with the "*uphini*". Do not make it too thick. Cover again with the lid and leave it to cook on a lower heat at this stage, "*imbiza*" the pot, "*iyatswinya*" or "*iyashinyila*", take off the lid and mix the food well.
- Put back the lid and leave another 4-5 minutes.
- Open the pot and again, mix well and then take off the heat.
- Serve into any type of plates, wooden, metal, ceramic, bowls or flat dishes.
- Serve.

07 ISITSHWALA

- Abantu bangadla ngamunye ngamunye kumbe ngamaqembu ejwayele ukuya ngobudala babantu kumbe ukuthi ngabayini, njengokuthi omama, obaba kumbe abantwana bodwa.
- Isitshwala sidliwa lesitshebo esingaba yinyama, imbida, izankefu zochago, idelele, imbuya, amakhowa, inhlanzi kumbe amacimbi.
- Isitshwala singaphekwa ngempuphu yomumbu, eyamabele, eyophoko kumbe eyenyawuthi.
- Imphuphu ingaba ngegayiswe esigayweni, echolwe ngelitshe lembokodo ngabe egigwe engigeni ngomgigo.
- Isitshwala yiyo ingqobo ingqungquthela yokudla kwakithi esintwini.
- Libambamuzi ngesiLungu abathi yi "*staple food*".
- Siyasuthisa siphe amandla siqinisu mzimba njalo.

Phendula Le Imibuzo

Q: Nxa amanzi esebila ngophehlo _____?

Q: Nxa sesijiyisa sibonda ngo _____?

Q: Esikucupha sisidla ngu _____?

Q: Isitshwala sidliwa le _____?

07 THICK PORRIDGE Continued

- This dish like all the others can be eaten by individuals or as groups from the same plates. The groups can be according to gender or age for example, a group of children mixed, then women alone and men also on their own.

- Thick porridge in Zimbabwe and other African countries, is always eaten with relish "*isitshebo*" like vegetables "*imbida*", meat "*inyama*", milk "*uchago*", fish "*inhlanzi*", maphane worms "*amacimbi*" or mushrooms "*amakhowa*".

- As we said, to prepare this vital dish one needs water and grain flour from either maize, sorghum, or any type of millet, "*impuphu*".

- The flour can be ground at the grinding mill or traditionally between two stones, the bigger stone called the "*ilitshe*" and the smaller stone, "*imbokodo*". Grain can also be put into and pounded in the wooden "*ingiga*", using the wooden stick or special pole "*umgigo*".

- This thick porridge, "*isitshwala*", is our principal traditional staple food. It is very filling and strengthening.

Answer These Questions

Q: When water boils, what do we do with "uphehlo" _____?

Q: To thicken, we mix with the _____?

Q: What are the lumps we take with our fingers as we eat this food _____?

Q: Thick porridge is always eaten together with _____?

08 AMAHEWU

- Amahewu yikudla okunathwayo njalo okuqakatheke kakhulu o esintwini.
- Amahewu enziwa kumbe avutshwe ngelambazi kumbe e ngesitshwala.
- Avutshelwa nge mithombo yophoko kumbe eyamabele.
- Kulezinsuku lefulawa isisenziwa imvubelo yamahewu.
- Khangela lapho esixoxe khona ngesitshwala ngaphezulu lalapho okuxoxwa khona ngokuphekwa kwelambazi ulandele kodwa ungacini usufaka ledobi kumbe ilemoni emahewini hayi.
- Cuba kumbe vuba isitshwala loba ilambazi osekupholile uthele amanzi eneleyo ukuthi kunatheke kungabi lula kakhulu.
- Phehla ke ngophehlo ubulale amapundu.
- Thela imvubelo yakho yemithombo kumbe ifulawa engaba yisilinganiso sokhezo lokudla kumbe ezimbili ezintathu kusiya ngobunengi bamahewu akho.
- Phehla kuhlangane.
- Thela ke embengeni kumbe eqhageni lamahewu nge nkomitsho kumbe ngenkezo yokukha amanzi.

08 GRAIN FLOUR DRINK

- This drink is called "*Amahewu*". In Zimbabwe, it is traditionally or culturally as common and as important as the traditional beer.

- It is prepared by mixing cold water, cold porridge or thick porridge, finger broken or smoothed and then adding fermentation flour "*imthombo*" from sorghum "*amabele*", finger millet "*uphoko*" or pearl millet "*inyawuthi*". Refer back to where we discussed the cooking of porridge and thick porridge before.

- People also use the usual baking flour that we buy from shops, instead of "*imthombo*".

- Remember **not** to put lemon, butter or peanut butter to the porridge that you are using to make this drink.

- Beat and stir porridge until smooth or until only small lumps remain if using thick porridge. Bring it to a nice drinkable thickness by adding water. Add fermentation flour, it can be a teaspoon or larger spoonful depending on how much drink you have made.

- Pour the drink into an appropriate container, traditionally a calabash "*imbenge*" using a cup or the long handle gourd "*inkezo*".

08 AMAHEWU

- Nxa uthela embodleleni, woba lalokhu abathi yi, "*funnel*" ukuze ungachithi.
- Vala imbenge loba siphi isiphathelo osisebenzi sileyo ngento ehlanzekileyo.
- Ngakusisa esebilile amahewu, asenganathwa usebenza, uziphumulela, liyimuli kumbe libanengi linxusene njengezakhamizi omakhelwana kulelima.
- Ilima lingaba ngeloku hlakula, ukubiya, ukubhula, ukubhada, ukweluka amathikili lesihlothi, liqunta amazambane loba ukudobhindumba.
- Hawu kuhlatshelwe ingoma zamalima kubemnandi kunathwa lawo mahewu.

Phendula Le Imibuzo

Q: Qamba okubili okoku vubela amahewu ukuze abile.

Q: Amahewu angaphekwa kunxuswe abantu kulani?

Q: Nxa sisenza amahewu singavuba _____ kumbe _____?

Q: Amahewu kawadliwa enziwani?

08 GRAIN FLOUR DRINK Continued

- If you are pouring the drink into a bottle, then it is better to use a funnel.
- Close or cover the container with a clean lid or some fabric.
- The following day, the drink should be ready. You can drink alone, or as a family and friends resting, or with neighbours that you have invited "*ukunxusa abantu*" to come and help you with some work "*lisebenza*" at home "*ngekhaya*", or in the fields "*emasimini*" which we call "*ilima*". "*lima*" can be for cultivating "*ukuhlakula*", threshing "*ukubhula*", fencing "*ukubiya*" weaving or tying roofing grass "*liseluka amathikili kumbe isihlothi lokubopha utshani*". You could also be working on a mud hut or house "*lisakha kumbe libhada indlu*" or harvesting "*livuna*" any crop in the fields like peanuts "*amazambane*", beans or peas "*indumba*" or roundnuts "*indlubu*".
- People sing various work related songs, "*ingoma*", while doing each of these activities "*besebenza*" enjoying traditional drinks like "*amahewu*" and or beer "*utshwala*", which ever they are comfortable with.

Answer These Questions

Q: Name two types of fermentation powders, flour, used traditionally for this drink _____ , _____ ?

Q: "Amahewu" can be prepared a day before, when you want to invite people which we call _____ for what activities?

Q: To initially prepare this drink, the ingredients are _____ and _____ ?

Q: You do not eat "amahewu," instead you _____ it.

09 AMAQEBELENGWANE

- Amaqebelengwane ngingathi yisinkwa kumbe amabhanzi amnandi esintu.
- Aphekwa ngempuphu yomumbu loba eyamabele kumbe eyenyawuthi.
- Hlanganisela esiphathelweni esiyingubhe impuphu letshukela lesawudo elizwela kangcinyane njengokuthanda kwakho.
- Thela amanzi aqandayo mbijana mbijana uvubanise kujiye.
- Cupha inhlanganiso le ubumbabumbe zandla zombili imisuba engaba ngange ngqindi yakho.
- Faka embizeni eseziko elamanzi asekhudumala angaphezudlwana kwemisuba yakho yokuqala.
- Umlilo ubengolingeneyo nje.
- Qhubeka usendlala imisuba le kuhle kuhle iziphele inhlanganiso yakho
- Sibekela imbiza wekele kuxhwathe kuhle kuhle kungatsheli.
- Nxa kuphela amanzi ubona kungaka vuthisisisi, thela amanye amanzi akhudumalayo kumbe atshisayo wekele kuvuthwe.
- Ungabona esevuthiwe amaqebelengwana akho, yephula imbiza eziko.
- Phakulula kudliwe sekuphola pholile.
- Dlanini liphelekezelisa ngetiye loba omunye nje umhlobo wokunathwayo kodwa hatshi amahewu. Lokho Phela kuyabe sekuyiku nathisa impuphu ngempuphu.

Phendula Le Imibuzo

Q: Sithela amanzi anjani ekuvubeni amaqebelengwane?
_____.

Q: Njenge mbambayila amaqebelengwane amnandi usidla u _____ okokwehlisa.

37

09 TRADITIONAL BOILED DUMPLINGS

- "*Amaqebelengwane*" are like the buns, scones or tortillas found in other cultures. They are cooked using water and maize, sorghum or millet flour "*impuphu*".
- Mix the ingredients in a bowl depending on how many you want to make. Add enough sugar and a little salt to taste.
- Pour on warm water and mix together with clean bare hands.
- Knead the thick dough and then, taking pieces the size of your fist or smaller, mould them as you would when making meatballs.
- Over a medium heat, put these pieces into the pot that is already on the stove with hot water.
- Have enough water to cover the first layer.
- Wait a few seconds after every layer to prevent the sticking together of the balls in each layer.
- Continue the process till you finish the dough.
- Cover the pot or saucepan with a lid and leave to cook slowly.
- You can pour a little more hot water if need be.
- When satisfactorily cooked, take the pot off the heat.
- Serve.
- You can drink tea or any other drink you like while eating this dish, but not "*amahewu*". To drink "*amahewu*" while eating "*amaqebelengwane*" would be like accompanying mealie meal with itself, which would be tasteless and not really proper.

Answer These Questions

Q: What water do we pour when mixing ingredients for this dish _____?

Q: Just like sweet potatoes, "*imbambayila*", this dish is eaten with a _____? Otherwise you would choke and not enjoy the tasty food.

10 INKOBE

- Inkobe ziyimihlobo etshiyeneyo kusiya ngesilimo okhethe ukusipheka.
- Ungapheka isilimo sibe sinye kumbe uzidibanise njengokuthi uhlanganisa indlubu lamazambane kumbe amazambane lendumba.
- Kanengi isilimo sihlanganiswa lomumbu ohululiweyo loba ukuthi umumbu ophekiweyo wonyiswa, ufutho phela.
- Pheka amagwadla kuqala okwesikhathi esingaba yimizuzu engamatshumi amabili ngoba wona alukhuni ayaphuza ukuvuthwa.
- Thelake phakathi isilimo nxa imbiza ivele inkulu.
- Ngezelela amanzi usibekeli mbiza uyekele kuxhwathe kuzekuvuthwe.
- Ungabona amanzi esemalutshwana kungaka vuthisisisi, thela amanye amanzi atshisayo kuqhubeke kuxhwathe.
- Thela amanzi atshisayo.ngaso sonke isikhathi omele uhlale ulawo eceleni.
- Indlubu nxa zilamakhasi, uyazitshokola ukuzigigagiga engigeni ngomgigo zingacezuki kodwa zihlubeke amakhasi.
- Khiphela esitsheni ubusucupha nganlutshwane uziphephethe ngokhomane upese ukhethe yonkingcekeza ungakazi theli embizeni. Lendumba ezilamakhasi uqala wenze njalo.
- Nxa amazambane elamakhasi, uwacacade uhlungule uphephethe ngokhomane ukhiphe amakhasi ukhethe ingcekeza yonke.

10 MIXTURE OF DRY MAIZE KERNELS AND DRY LEGUMINOUS SEEDS

- This traditional dish has several various varieties.
- You vary the dishes by mixing different legume ingredients, for example, peanuts, peas, beans or roundnuts with "*amagwadla*", boiled maize kernels from the recipe that we discussed before. The kernels could be ones we call "*ufutho*" preboiled soft maize, corn which was then dried to preserve for off-season. Samp, skinless kernels can also be used instead of just dry maize kernels.
- Boil the maize first for about 15-20 minutes before adding the other ingredients because it takes longer to cook. Not Samp though because it has been cracked and peeled so is already softer. Wash the ingredients thoroughly before cooking.
- If the pot is big enough, add the legume or legumes you have chosen to cook.
- Cover the pot and let the food cook.
- Have hot water nearby so as to keep adding more if the water gets low. You should never add cold water.
- If the nuts are still in their pods, shell them by pounding them slightly to remove "*amakhasi*", the skin.
- Do the same with both beans or peas. After pounding or shelling them, winnow to remove chaff and pick out any other debris.

10 INKOBE

- Akulanto embi njengenkobe ezilamatshe ezilumelayo. Yikho kule nkulumo eyilizwi elihlakaniphileyo ethi, Yebo ungenzenje, kusasa kuyizolo, uzafika lawe lapho engikhona ngikuphekele ezilamatshe. Uyabe esonga ukuthi uzaphindisela ngokukudlisa ezizakulimaza amazinyo inkobe.

- Uma sezizavuthwa inkobe, faka isawudo obona ukuthi lizazwela.

- Zingavuthwa inkobe, yephuli mbiza uphakulule kudliwe.

- Ungazidla inkobe unathisa ngamanzi kodwa zilunge kakhulu kudliwe unathisa ngokutshisayo okunjenge tiye phela.

- Ukunatha itiye usidla inkobe kuhle kakhulu ngoba kwenza isisu singagubelani siqumbelane sibelomoya okuyinto ehlupha abanengi ngenkobe.

- Inkobe ziqakatheke kakhulu phakathi komuzi esintwini.

- Ziyasuthisa lokuqinisa amasotsha omzimba ziphe lamandla.

- Yikudla okulomswane.

- Njengoba sitshilo phambilini, ukuthela amanzi aqandayo ekudleni okuphekwayo, kuyagwanyisa ukudla kunabe kungazabe kusavuthwa kuhle inkobe zibelalo mqhumuzo.

10 DRY LEGUMINOUS SEEDS Continued

- There is no worst eating experience than having this dish with small stones or sand particles "*amatshe*" in it.
- When a person swears "*ukusonga*" to take revenge, especially ladies, they will say, oh you are doing this to me! Ok, you will find me at my own place where I will be married and I will cook for you one with sand particles or stones. Saying "*uzaku phekela ezilamatshe*", they will also give you a hard time. This is because chewing food with sand in it is painful and very uncomfortable.
- When the food is nearly cooked, add enough salt to taste.
- Leave to cook about 8 more minutes then take off the heat and serve. Let the people dig in and enjoy.
- You can have this food with any drink you like but, "*inkobe*" are best eaten with a hot drink like tea.
- Having this food with a hot drink is good for your stomach. It helps prevent constipation and other digestive discomforts that cause wind, feeling gassy or bloated. This is a problem that many find relief from this key traditional dish.
- This dish is second to "*isitshwala*" in importance traditionally, in a Zimbabwean home at least.
- They are very filling, "*zilomswane inkobe*".
- They are good for the body's immune system "*amasotsha omzimba*". It has nutrients like protein and carbohydrates for energy and protection.
- Each dish is named after the leguminous ingredient in it. Like "*inkobe zendlubu*" the roundnut dish, and "*inkobe zamazambane*" the peanut dish "*inkobe zendumba"* the cowpeas or bean dish.
- It is important to emphasise that while this food is cooking, always add hot or boiling water not cold water because it hardens the food, causing it not to cook properly.

10 INKOBE

Phendula Le Imibuzo

Q: Qamba imhlobo yenkobe ongazipheka.

Q: Ngaphandle kwama gwadla, yiwuphi omunye umumbu ophekwa lenkobe?

Q: Ukuze ungaqumbelani, kumele wenzeni nxa usidla inkobe?

Q: Ongathokozi ngokumphatha kwakho angathi uzaku phekela inkobe ezinjani?

10 DRY LEGUMINOUS SEEDS Continued

Answer These Questions

Q: Name different mixtures of ingredients for various dishes of "inkobe".

Q: Besides "amagwadla", which other types of maize kernels are added to the legumes for this food.

Q: To prevent constipation or indigestion problems like gas, what should you have with this dish.

Q: If someone is not happy with how you are treating them, they usually say they will cook what kind of "inkobe" for you when you come to theirs?

11 AMAKHOWA

- Amakhowa ayimihlobo eminengi njalo ayisitshebo esiqakathekileyo.
- Amanye amnandi ayadliwa kanti akhona ayingozi abulalayo.
- Abulalayo isibonelo yila athiwa yinkowane kumbe inkowankowane.
- Ungabokukha amakhowa ekhaya, ensimini, kumbe egangeni ngaphandle kokuba ufundisiwe njalo uleqiniso ukuthi angadliwayo sibisibili.
- Buza, uthathe ithuba elide ufunda ngomehluko wamakhowa.
- La alinywayo athengiswa ezitolo akhanya esazakala engelangozi.
- Amakhowa aphekwa emanzi kumbe esechayiwe onyiswa.
- Eminye imihlobo yamakhowa yile: aweziduli, inhowa, inetsi, isibindi senja, isinankamtshetshe, ubudzugwe, ubutshabitshabi, indlebe kagogo, indevu zikababamkhulu, idindindi, idondowa.
- Khana ke amakhowa uqume ulahle impande ezilenhlabathi.
- Sikelela ayabe emakhulu njengawesiduli ubusugezisa uphindaphinde.
- Ugezise emanzini amanengi ukuze amakhowa andende ukhethe ingcekeza endenda lawo enjengotshani lamahlamvu.
- Lokhu njalo ukwenzela ukuthi inhlabathi inikame isale phansi nxa ukhipha amakhowa.
- Khipha amakhowa uwachaye nxa ezadliwa sewomile.

11 MUSHROOMS

- Mushrooms come in many varieties and they are one of the most important ingredients of our traditional relish dishes.
- Some are edible "*ayadliwa*", nice and tasty but there are those that are poisonous and very dangerous.
- The example of the poisonous ones are the "*inkowane/inkowankowane*".
- Never go and collect mushrooms around the home "*ngekhaya*", in the fields "*emasimini*" or in the forest, desert of bush "*egangeni*" alone or with others until you have been taught thoroughly and are confident enough to remember which ones are edible and which ones are not.
- Therefore, it is vital to study seriously and learn the important differences between the different types.
- The mushrooms we buy from shops are generally safe because they have been tested and tasted.
- Mushrooms can be cooked fresh "*emanzi*", or from dried "*echayiwe awoma*".
- One popular type of mushroom is found around anthills and termite hills in the forest "*aweziduli*". Other varieties are "*inhowa, inetsi, isibindi senja*", "dogliver", "*Isinanga mutshetshe, ubudzugwe, ubutsabitsabi, indlebe kagogo*", "Grandma's ear", "*indevu zikababamkhulu*", "Granddaddy's beard", "i*dindindi*" and "i*dondowa*".
- Pick the mushrooms and cut away the dirty root tips.
- Slice into desired shapes and sizes. Wash the mushrooms more than once in plenty of water so that they float out the debris like grass "*utshani*" and leaves "*amahlamvu*", while sand "*inhlabathi*" settles "*inikame*" at the bottom of the bowl.
- Throw away the grass, leaves and any other debris.
- Remove the clean mushrooms with your hands so that any left over sand particles and excess water will drain away between your fingers.
- If the mushrooms are being preserved for off season, spread them on a clean surface and leave to dry in a cool area.

11 AMAKHOWA

- Nxa ephekwa emanzi, afake embizeni eseziko elamanzi atshisayo acina ngaphansanyana kwengaphezulu yamakhowa ubunengi.

- Yekela axhwathe aze avuthwe ubusu faka isawudo ugoqozele ledobi ngabe ulaza kumbe uwakhanzinge ngamafutha okupheka.

- Nxa ufaka ulaza, yekela amanzi aphele kumbe uwacenge ubusuthela ke ulaza uphenduphendule ngophini usibekelele kuhlale kancane uphinde uphendule uzusuthiseke ukuthi sekuvuthwe kahle.

- Awedobi, akhiphe amakhowa embizeni kusale isobho.

- Goqozela idobi eleneleyo ufake loba yini enambithekisayo oyifunayo olayo.

- Yekela ibundubundu leli lixhwathe imizuzu engaba mine.

- Buyisela ke amakhowa akho embizeni uphendule kuhlangane.

- Sibekelela uyekele kuxhwathe ndawonye ube uphendula unanzelela kungatsheli. Uzwe lokuthi isawudo lizwele kuhle.

- Ngemuva kwemizuzu engaba mihlanu, phendula wephule isitshebo kudliwe lesitshwala. Uyaziquma ulimi nxa ungananzelele.

- Amakhowa angaphekwa ke langoku wakhazinga ngamafutha kufakwe ohanyanisi, amatomatisi lokunye okunambithekisayo.

11 MUSHROOMS *Continued*

- If the mushrooms are being cooked while fresh, put them in the pot with water that is just a bit below the top of them.
- Let them cook enough and add a pinch of salt. If peanut butter "*idobi*" is to be added, dissolve a spoonful or two of it in hot water in a cup first. When smooth, pour the peanut butter into the pot and mix well.
- If adding cream "*ulaza*", make sure the mushrooms are cooked, dry or drain out the water "*cenga amanzi*", fiost. Do the same if you are frying them in cooking oil "*amafutha*". Add the cream or oil and keep stirring to mix well and prevent burning.
- Add also the spices of your choice. It could be paprika "*ibilebile*" to give it a kick.
- When adding peanut butter, the other method is to remove the mushrooms and leave the broth in the pot. Put the peanut butter into the pot and stir it in until it is smooth. Check salt and add your other spices, mix to desired thickness and then cover the pot.
- Let it simmer for about 4-5 minutes. Open and put the mushrooms back into the pot. Mix them well with the simmering peanut butter.
- Put the lid back on and continue simmering. Stir occasionally and check the taste.
- After about 5 minutes, stir well and take off the heat. Serve this delicious relish to go with the staple dish "*isitshwala*".
- The joke often said about this delicious combination is that you will surely accidentally bite your tongue "*uzaziluma ulimi*", you will be enjoying the meal so much that, your mind will relax and forget what is in your mouth and be chewing when you should not be.
- Like other dishes, when using cooking oil especially, you can add fresh onion "*ihanyanisi*", tomatoes "*amatamatisi*", red, green or yellow peppers, parsley, garlic for the relish to be aromatic, appetising and even tastier.

48

11 AMAKHOWA

Phendula Le Imibuzo

Q: Qamba imihlobo yamakhowa obalengayo ibemithathu.

Q: Qamba isibonelo samakhowa ayingozi abulalayo.

Q: Oyadinga amakhowa sithi uya _____.

11 MUSHROOMS Continued

Answer These Questions

Q: Name any three types "imihlobo" of mushrooms "yamakhowa" you read "obale" about, "ngayo" _____, _____, _____

Q: Name an example of poisonous mushrooms _____

Q: When one is going to fetch mushrooms traditionally we say "uya _____, _____".

12 IDOBI

- Idobi lenziwa ngamazambane acacadiweyo, akhanzingwa, acholwa kumbe agigwa. Liphekwa lemibhida emanzi ngabe ewonyisiweyo yabayimfushwa.

- Liphekwa njalo lenyama echaywe yoma imihwabha phela kumbe egigiweyo iswayi. Limnandi njalo idobi liphekwe lamakhowa kumbe lelambazini, esinkweni loba enopini isijeza phelake leso.

- Cacada amazambane obona ezakwenela isitshebo sakho.

- Ahlungule ngokhomane ukhiphe amakhasi ukhethe lengcekeza.

- Faka udengezi eziko uwakhanzinge angatshi.

- Nxa esepholile, agigagige engigeni ngomgigo wakho ohlanzekileyo uhlube amakhasi.

- Khipha uphephethe ngokhomane ukhiphe okuhlubekileyo.

- Ungawabisela engigeni uwagige abeyimpuphu ungakawacholi.

- Chola amazambane elitsheni ngembokodo uphindaphinde aze ancincime.

- Abanye bathanda idobi elicholwa lisale ligayekile. Kukuwe ke lokho.

12　PEANUT BUTTER

- Peanut butter is made from shelled peanuts "*amazambane acacadiweyo*". These are roasted "*ayakhanzingwa*", pounded "*agigwe*" a little to remove the skins "*izikhumba*" and then ground "*acholwe*". You can pound them again first to a powder, and then grind them smooth or crunchy between the two special stones kept for this.

- Peanut butter is an important ingredient for relish dishes like dried vegetables "*imfushwa*", dry meat "*imhwabha*" and mushrooms "*amakhowa*".

- It is also good to spread on bread or eat with porridge and "*inopi*".

- Shell enough of them for the purpose if they have dried in their pods.

- Remove the chaff and roast them until crisp. Let them cool and then pound them slightly, just to remove the skins.

- Remove all chaff and other debris.

- You can then pound them again before grinding or grind straight away with the usual special stones.

- It is one's choice to make it smooth, or leave it a little crunchy.

12 IDOBI

- Khipha inyama, imibhida kumbe amakhowa akho esevuthiwe embizeni.
- Goqozela idobi esobheni esembizeni ufake lesawudo elingazwela.
- Sibekela imbiza uyekele kuxhwathe okwemizuzu engaba mine.
- Phendula ubusubuyisela okukhiphileyo embizeni uphendule kuhlangane kahle uzwe lesawudo ufake ibilebile lokunye okuthandayo.
- Sibekela imbiza uyekele kuxwathe imizuzu engaba yisithupha kusiya kwelitshumi uma imbiza inkulu. Ube uphendula ukuze idobi lingatsheli.
- Yephula ke imbiza uphakulule kudliwe. Lesi yisitshebo esimnandi okwamagama nxa usidla lesitshwala. Uthola okhekhe sebekhotha iminwe bazebakhothe lengalo.

Phendula Le Imibuzo

Q: Nxa sihluba amazambane emakhasini sithi Siya _____?

Q: Ukukhipha amazambane esihlahlanyaneni sawo yikwenzani?

Q: Idobi licholwa ngembokodo e _____?

12 PEANUT BUTTER *Continued*

- If adding to a dish, remove the meat "*inyama*", vegetables "*imbida*" or mushrooms "*amakhowa*", from the pot when well cooked, leave just the broth, "*umhluzi*".
- Stir in the peanut butter and add enough salt to taste.
- Add any other ingredients for seasoning that you like.
- Cover the pot and let it cook for about 4-5 minutes.
- Open and stir and then put back what you took out before, meat, vegetables or mushrooms. Check the taste and put more of anything needed. Let it cook for about 6-10 minutes but keep stirring at short intervals.
- Take off the heat. Serve with whatever you have as the main dish.
- This is a very tasty traditional relish dish that goes well with the staple dish, thick porridge, "*isitshwala*".

Answer These Questions

Q: When removing peanuts from their pods we say you are _____?

Q: What do we call removing peanuts from the plant?

Q: Peanut butter is ground using stones called _____ and _____?

13 AMACIMBI

- Amacimbi agolwa ezihlahleni ezinjenga maphane lamagonde lezinye ezaziwayo ezigabeni. Avela emavevaneni. Angaphekwa adliwe emanzi kumbe aphekwe achaywe ome kuqala.
- Gola amacimbi ubone angakoneli izigqoko.
- Akhame aphume ingcekeza yangaphakathi uwagezise.
- Aphekeke ufake isawudo uhle uwenze isitshebo emanzi kumbe uwachaye njengoba sengitshilo ngaphezulu.
- Nxa esevuthiwe akhiphe embizeni ukhudumeze amafutha ufake okuthandayo okokunambithekisa ohanyanisi ubusuwabisela ukhanzinge.
- Wothi nje qwa amanzana uqhubeke ukhanzinga.
- Abanye bathanda ukuwadla enjalo engalasobho kanti abanye bayawafaka lamatamatisi abelesojanyana.
- Ungathi klu amanzi azandende nje amacimbi esojeni ecwayizayo inkanyezana hayi isobho kayijiye ibelutshwana okwenela abazakudla.
- Nxa ufuna awedobi, akhiphe embizeni kusale umsobho. Goqozela idobi uliyekele lixhwathaxhwathe.
- Buyisela amacimbi uphenduphendule uzwe isawudo. Idobi kumbe isobho kumele kujiye kungabi ngamanzi amantshululu hatshi.

13 AMAPHANE / MOPANE WORMS

- "*Amaphane*" worms are collected in the wild from trees especially "*emaphaneni*", the drought resistant trees that grow mainly in the south west, west and north west of Zimbabwe and some neighbouring countries.
- They are a product of butterflies and can either be eaten fresh or boiled slightly in salty water and dried to preserve them for the off-season.
- Collect these edible caterpillars with care and protective garments because they can badly stain your clothes. Mind the prickly spikes too.
- Squeeze out the gut and wash them thoroughly.
- Boil them in salt and eat them either fresh as a snack or as a relish, or dry them as a future ingredient or a snack.
- If eating them fresh, cook them in hot water until tender adding small amounts of hot water if it gets low. Then, fry until crispy in cooking oil adding onion and any other seasonings of your choice.
- Some people like to eat them with gravy but others prefer them dry, crunchy and crispy.
- If you cook them in too much water, making them float in the watery gravy, they will not taste nice at all. Make them appetising in thick well seasoned gravy.
- If cooking them with peanut butter, take them out of the pot when well cooked. Add peanut butter to the broth in the pot, stir until smooth and fairly thick. Cover.
- Let it simmer for 5 minutes and then put the worms back into the pot, mix, add salt plus your spices if desired and then cover.

Continued

13 AMACIMBI

- Yekela kuxhwathe imizuzu engaba ngalombili emlilweni olingeneyo kodwa ube usibukula uphendula ukuze kungatsheli.
- Yephula ke imbiza uphakulule kudliwe.
- Nxa ephekiwe afakwa isawudo esesemanzi onyiswa, amnandi udobha uzidlela nje ebusika enjalo ewodwa. Alemali amacimbi ekuthengiseni ngoba kawatholakali kuzozonke izigaba zelizwe. Atholakala kakhulu ezigabeni ezilamaphane njenge Khezi, Plumtree, Tsholotsho.
- Malutshwane kubo Nkayi, Mzola, Filabhusi lezinyi indawo.
- Yikho uthola abantu bewahaba emamakethe besiyawa thengisa kibo lapho angatholakali kakhulu khona.

Phendula Le Imibuzo

Q: Obamba amacimbi kuthiwa wenzani?

Q: Yisiphi isihlahla esithandwa ngamacimbi kakhulu?

Q: Amacimbi aphenduka abengama.

Q: Kuyini okubili okwenza abantu besabe ukubamba amacimbi?

Fun Exercise:
Ngomunwe lingisela ukuhamba kwecimbi.

13 WORMS Continued

- Leave it to cook for about 8 more minutes on a low heat stirring every about 2 minutes.
- Remove the pot from the heat and dish up. Serve and let people enjoy this delicacy.
- If, on the other hand, the worms were boiled briefly in salty water and left to dry, as we said, they make a good snack just picking and eating later like popcorn.
- These worms are a great source of finance for many families because they are not found in most areas of our country. They are mainly found in areas like Khezi, Plumtree and Tsholotsho.
- There are fewer in places like Nkayi, Mzola or Filabhuzi and others.
- As a result, you find people queuing to buy or order them from markets, to then go and sell them in their own districts or to go and sell them in other countries.

Answer These Questions

Q: What do we say someone harvesting the maphane worms is doing?

Q: Which tree, "isihlahla" is mainly liked by these worms?

Q: The caterpillars turn into what if they remain in the forest?

Q: What two things make people fear to catch "maphane" worms?

Fun Exercise:
Using your finger, imitate the way "amacimbi" move.

14 AMATHANGA LA MAKHOMANE

- Amathanga lamakhomane yikudla okumnandi kwemasimini okwentanga ezinabayo njenge zekhabe kumbe njengedumba.
- Intanga zamathanga imilibo yazo emincinyane yiyo esiyikha ibeyimibhida yebhobola sitshebe ngayo imanzi kumbe ingumfushwa isiwomile.
- Dinga ukhethe ithanga eselivuthiwe elingasilo klabhuzi.
- Nxa lilikhomane, dinga elibuthakathaka elingomanga ukukomba phela.
- Sikelela incezwana ezilingeneyo zethanga kumbe ikhomane, ukhiphe intanga ethangeni.
- Beka imbiza eziko emlilweni omnenganyana.
- Thela amanzi akhudumalayo kumbe atshisayo avala incezu zokuqala eziphansi embizeni.
- Yendlala ingzezu zakho zonke embizeni.
- Sibekela imbiza ngesidekiselo kuvaleke ngci ukuze amakhomane angabi yimigwili. Yekela axhwathe aze avuthwe amathanga kumbe amakhomane akho kodwa angavuthwa edlulise.
- Ungawadla ewodwa nje enjalo kumbe uwavube ngochago uzitike isisu sicwazimule. Abaziyo bathi ayikudla okusiza emehlweni amathanga.

14 PUMPKINS AND GOURDS

- Pumpkin and gourd dishes are a vital part of our traditional foods.
- They are grown in fields or in gardens by sowing seeds which germinate and spread as vines, like melons and then bear the fruit.
- The tender, smaller fore leaves of pumpkin vines can be eaten as a vegetable fresh or dry.
- Choose a fully grown, firm, ripe pumpkin, not a too tender one.
- On the other hand, the gourd should be tender enough that your finger nail goes through.
- Cut into medium size pieces removing seeds in the pumpkins.
- Have the pot on a medium heat .
- Pour hot or boiling water to just cover the base of the pot.
- Lay all the pieces in the pot and then cover tightly with the lid so the food will cook well.
- Let them cook until tender being careful not to overcook.
- You can eat this food as it is or mix with some fresh milk and enjoy. They are quite filling.
- Experts often say the yellow in the pumpkin is very good for the eyes.

14 AMATHANGA LA MAKHOMANE

Phendula Le Imibuzo

Q: Kuyini okukhulu ithanga lekhomane eselikhule laqedela?

Q: Iziqa ezisikelelwa zifakwe mbizeni sithi kuyini?

Q: Ikhomane eselomile elingasa phekekiyo kuthiwa selinjani?

Q: Zizalwa yini lezi izilimo?

Q: Bawathwala ngani omama amakhomane bevela wakha?

14 PUMPKINS AND GOURDS *Continued*

Answer These Questions

Q: Which is bigger usually a fully grown pumpkin and a ripe gourd that can be cooked.

Q: What do we call the pieces that we cut out and cook?

Q: A dry gourd that has dried out and can no longer be cooked is said to be what?

Q: What brings forth or bears the pumpkin or the gourd?

Q: What are the special traditional weaker straw woven baskets women use to carry pumpkins and gourds or maize from the fields?

15 ISAHLAKA ISATHUBI LESATHIYANE

- Inkomokazi esanda kuzala ilochango olunonekakhulu ngolaza "*cream*".
- Loluchago lwendlezane I "*colostrum*" sithi kalukahlambuluki, kaluka lungeli ukudliwa. Kalumhlophe hatshi lusa ganu, sathanga.
- Luchago oluqinisa umzimba wenkonyane yikho liyekelwa okwensuku ezingabane lizimunyela unina ingasengwa.
- Ngosuku lwesihlanu, sekungasengwa abafana bapheke isahlaka sabo khonangale ezibayeni badlele khonangale futhi.
- Isahlaka ke amankazana ayasizila kawasidli yikho abafana beziphekela badlele esibayeni.
- Uchago luphekwa lulodwa luzijiyele kudliwe.
- Ngemva kwensuku ezimbili kumbe ezintathu, kusengwa inkomokazi kuphekwe isathiyane isathubi phela.

15 MILK DISHES - COLOSTRUM & WHOLE MILK

- Soon after calving, a cow's milk "*uchago lwenkomokazi*" is very creamy and rich called colostrum.
- This new mother "*indlezane*" produces milk that is said not to be good for human consumption yet.
- It is not white, "*kalumhlophe*" or "*hatshi*", it is yellowish cream, "*lusathanga, saganu*".
- It is very good for strengthening "*ukuqinisathe*", the calf. It has all the necessary nutrients needed for them. That is why the cow is not usually milked at that stage for about 4 days "*insuku ezine*", so that the calf may have enough of this colostrum milk.
- After this, about the fifth day, traditionally the herd boys milk the cow and cook the milk by the corrals on their own.
- This special dish of milk, coagulating as they heat it, is called "*isahlaka*".
- This is a dairy dish that is taboo for girls and women. That is why the cooking and eating is done by the corrals, not in the home.
- The milk is not mixed with any other ingredient.
- After about 2 to 3 days of cooking "*isahlaka*", the milk is then used to cook another very popular delicious dish called "*isathiyane*", also called "*isathubi*".

15 ISAHLAKA ISATHUBI LESATHIYANE

- Isathubi siphekwa ngochago oselumhlophe osoluhlambulukile.
- Singaphekwa nje langochago lwenkomokazi emunyisa iguqa.
- Uthela uchago embizeni esiseziko emlilweni olingeneyo.
- Ungayimbokothi imbiza ngoba kumele unanzelele uchago lungabili luphuphumele eziko.
- Uchago lungachithekela eziko, inkomokazi iyadabuka imbele izwe ubuhlungu nxa ithole limunya kumbe uyisenga.
- Lokhu kuyenza ibelolaka ifune ukukhaba lokuhlaba ikuswelise ke isitshebo ilambise lenkonyane.
- Nxa uchago selutshisela ukubila embizeni, faka impuphu kancane kancane ugoqozele wenze ilambazi elijiye sakuthanda kwakho.
- Sibekela imbiza uyekele ixhwathe ulimuke ingatsheli ubuphendula ngemuva kemizuzwana engaba mine kumbe emithathu.
- Kungavuthwa, yephula imbiza uphakulule kudliwe laloba ngubani.
- Ngakho isathubi lilambazi nje eliphekwa ngochago lempuphu hatshi amanzi lempuphu.

15 MILK DISHES Continued

- The dish "*isathubi/isathiyane*" is prepared with two ingredients, fresh whole milk and maize *mealie* meal.
- To make it one uses fresh milk from when the calf is about 5 or 6 days old or more. As long as it is still suckling, and the cow is being milked, the milk can be used. It no longer matters how old the calf is.
- Pour the milk into the pot and boil it on a medium heat.
- Do not cover but stay close to the pot "*ungayi mbokothi imbiza*". This is because you have to watch that the milk does not boil and boil over, spilling onto the open fire or on the stove.
- Culturally, you are taught that if the milk spills into the fire, the cow's udder and teats will crack or tear causing it great pain when the calf tries to suck and when people try to milk it.
- It causes the cow to be angry "*iyazonda ibelolaka*" and kick or try to fight you with its horns "*ikuhlabe*". This starves the calf and deprives people of milk for tea, coffee or relish.
- When the milk gets hot, and not at boiling point, add the *mealie* meal "*impuphu*" bit by bit "*kangcane kangcane*" and stir continuously to be porridge like and to the thickness you like.
- Cover and leave to cook about 15 minutes making sure it is not burning. It can be checked and stirred every 3-4 minutes.
- When satisfactorily cooked, remove from fire or stove and serve to let everyone enjoy.
- So, "*isathubi*" is another kind of porridge traditionally cooked with just fresh milk and *mealie* meal, no water added. It can be eaten at any time of the day.

15 ISAHLAKA ISATHUBI LESATHIYANE

Phendula Le Imibuzo

Q: Indlezane esandakuzala inga sengwa kuphekwani?

Q: Yibaphi abazila ukudla isahlaka?

Q: Siphekelwa njalo sidlelwe ngaphi isahlaka?

Q: Isathubi siphekwa ithole linganani?

Q: Chaza ukuthi kungani uchago lungamelanga luchithekele kumbe lubilele eziko.

15 MILK DISHES Continued

Answer These Questions

Q: What do we call the dish cooked with colostrum as the only ingredient?

Q: Who in the family are not supposed to eat this delicacy?

Q: Where is it prepared and eaten?

Q: How old should the calf be for the cow's milk to be used to cook "Isathiyane/isathubi"

Q: Explain why milk should not be left to boil and spill off onto the open fire.

16 UMCABA

- Umcaba uphothulwa ngezankefu zamasi zihlanganiswe lohayezi.
- Uhayezi ngamabele bele aphekiweyo acholwa elitsheni ngembokodo asale engani agayekile.
- Uchago oluse siganwini ithunga phela, luthele esiphathelwe lulale luvuthwa lube lihiqa. Nxa uthela ube usefa ngesefa kumbe ngelembu elihlanzekileyo ukhipha ingcekeza.
- Ngelanga elilandelayo yengula ulaza, "*cream*", oluphezulu ehiqeni.
- Ulaza lolu ungalwenza iphehla uluxhwathise ucenge uyekele kuphole kujiye kube ngumfuma.
- Ungafaka ulaza emibhideni lemakhoweni ukhanzingise samafutha okupheka njalo.
- Phehla ihiqa ngophehlo kube lubundubundu oluhle.
- Gezisa igula uvale umunge isikhala esingaphansi kwegula phela, ngengcotho.
- Thela uchago eguleni uvale.

16 THE MIXTURE OF CURD WITH BOILED & GROUND SORGHUM OR MILLET

- This dish is made by using sour milk with mainly sorghum and millet flour.
- Pour the fresh milk from the container you milked it into called "*isiganu/ithunga*" into the storage vessel through a clean cloth or a clean sieve to remove any debris. Keep in a cool place.
- By the end of the following day, scoop out the cream "*ulaza*" that has formed a layer at the top of the slightly coagulated milk "*ihiqa*".
- The cream can be used to make a body cream called "*umfuma*" by heating up into an oil like liquid which is then called "*iphehla*". Continue cooking it until there is a layer of oil forming at the top. Remove from the heat. Let it cool and then drip out the oil into a clean bottle or small tin, leaving the residue at the bottom.
- Throw away the residue.
- The oil will harden a little as it cools into what becomes a very good body cream. Some substances with a better smell can be added to that cream, otherwise it has a strange smell and can quickly attract flies.
- If not used for "*umfuma*", the cream is mainly used in cooking relish dishes of mushrooms and fresh or dried green leafy vegetables, in place of cooking oil. Traditionally, not with okra.
- So, after removing the cream, whip up the milk until smooth. You can add a bit of fresh milk to it and then mix.
- Pour this smooth "*ubundubundu*" milk into the special calabash called "*igula*" washed clean with cold and then hot water. The small opening "*umunge*" at the bottom of this vessel is plugged with the special tree glue called "*ingcotho*" that has been finger moulded into a small cone shape, before pouring in the milk.

Continued

16 UMCABA

- Lokhu yikho ukwetha amasi.
- Yekela kuseguleni insuku ezingaba mbili.
- Beka igula phezu kwegabha elikhulu, inkonxa kumbe isiganu.
- Khipha ingcotho ukuze umlaza untshaze uphume.
- Vala umunge njalo ubusuthela amasi asesele eguleni esiphathelweni esihlanzekileyo.
- Thathake impuphu yakho oyicholileyo eyohayezi.
- Hlanganisa izankefu zakho zamasi lempuphu le kuhle kuhle.
- Lokhu yikho okuthiwa yikuphothula umcaba.
- Ngensuku zezolo abantwana bebekhangezwa umcaba ezandleni bengazichupheli.
- Bebesidla ke abantwana zandlazombili ngoba vele wemukela ebadaleni ngezandla zombili sonke isikhathi ngomkhuba wesintu.
- Bekuyikudla okungadliwa nje nsukuzonke umcaba lo hayi belilivela kanci igugu eligezisi'nhliziyo.

16 CURD WITH BOILED SORGHUM *Continued*

- This process is called "*ukwetha amasi*". Cover the "*igula*" with a clean piece of wet material or if it has a small top opening, you can use a clean short kernelless cob as the lid.
- Leave the milk there for at least 2 days.
- Lift and place the "*gula*" on a clean container such that the opening at the bottom is in line with it.
- Remove the glue, "*ingcotho*" from "*umunge*" to allow the whey, "*umlaza*", to flow out into the bottom container.
- When fully drained, close that bottom hole again.
- Pour the hard fluffy curds, "*amasi*", also known as "*izankefu*" into a clean container.
- Mix the milk with the sorghum or millet rough flour, produced by briefly boiling the grain, leaving it to cool and then grinding it into a course powder.
- This is the process we call "*ukuphothula umcaba wamasi*".
- In olden days, we never just ate this dish on its own straight from the plate. As children, one was given "*umcaba*" with a wooden or metal spoon and you would always culturally, "*ngomkhuba weSintu*", as we did with everything, receive it egerly with both hands. You still ate with both hands licking it all away. The child would often finish and stretch both hands out to receive another scoop.
- "*Umcaba*" was a very rare "*ivela kanci*" and special traditional dish, a delicacy valued as settling the heart, "*inhliziyo*".

16 UMCABA

Phendula Le Imibuzo

Q: Kuyini amabele aphekelwa umcaba?

Q: Kuthiwa yikwenzani ukwenza umcaba?

Q: Qamba imihlobo embili yamabele abomvu.

Q: Iqhaga lamasi libizwa kuthiwe kuyini?

Q: Umunge uvalwa _____?

Q: Kudala abantwana babephiwa njani umcaba?

16 CURD WITH BOILED SORGHUM *Continued*

Answer These Questions

Q: What do we call sorghum or millet cooked and ground for making "umcaba" dish?

Q: What do we call the process of mixing the ingredients to prepare this dish?

Q: Name two types of red sorghum.

Q: What is the name of the calabash used for sour curds?

Q: What is used to close "umunge"?

Q: Describe how children ate "umcaba" long ago, " kudala".

17 IDELELE

- Okudingekayo: idelele, amanzi, isawudo, umlotha ocengiweyo loba isoda lamatamatisi le anyanisi lokunye okunambithekisayo lokunukelelisayo ngxa ufuna.
- Kuledelele lemasimini umdlothi ledelele leganga elezidakeni.
- Khana idelele lingabi lengcekeza yotshani lokunye.
- Bekimbiza eziko ibelamanzi amancinyane angaphasi kwalo idelele ubunengi.
- Thela isoda nyana elutshwana.
- Nxa ungelasoda, faka umlotha emanzini aqandayo angaba zinkomitsho ezimbili kusiya ngobunengi bedelele ubusugoqoza.
- Yekela kuhlale okwemizuzu engaba mihlanu kunikame kucengeke amanzi asalephézulu.
- Thela lamanzi omlotha enkomitshini kuhle kuhle, kungadungi okunikemeyo ubusuwa thela lawamanzi embizeni.
- Yekela amanzi atshise.

17 OKRA

- Ingredients - okra, whichever type, water, ash or bicarbonate soda, a tomato, onion and spices if you like them.
- Traditionally, there are two types of "*idelele*", one found in the fields called "*umdlothi*" which grows on its own then the other which is found in muddy areas "*ezidakeni*", called "*idelele lezidaka*".
- The other type of vegetable is the Zimbabwean spinach, "*imbuya*" which grows on its own in fields, gardens and around the home especially, by the corrals, .
- Harvest okra with care otherwise you might pick together with grass, leaves or small sticks and insects.
- Put the pot on the heat with a little water.
- When it starts boiling, add about half or quarter of a teaspoon of bicarbonate of soda.
- If you have no soda, you can take a cup or two of cold water with a bowl and add a spoonful or two of clean ashes.
- Leave this to settle for about 5 minutes. The heavier ash particles will settle at the bottom, "*ngaphansi*" and the clear water will be at the top, "*ngaphezulu*".
- Drain the water slowly and carefully, pouring it into the pot. You can use a small strainer.
- Let the water boil.
- Add in the washed okra and stir well.
- Leave the pot open because okra can bubble up and spill over, "*ukululuma/ukuphuphuma*". If you are cooking the seed type okra, wash it and cut it finely first.
- Leave to cook.

Continued

17 IDELELE

- Thela idelele ugoqogoqoze.
- Yekela kuxhwathe imbiza ingasibekelwanga ngoba idelele liba legwebu eliluluma liphuphume.
- Woba uphendula ngemva kwesikhatshana ufake isawudo lokunye olakho okuhambelanayo nxa ufuna.
- Ngemuva kwemizuzu engaba litshumi, nxa usuthiseke ukuthi sekuvuthiwe, yephula imbiza eziko uphakulule.
- Idelele yisitshebo esimnandi umaginyisa amathe. Lakha umzimba ligeze lenhliziyo ingabi mnyama.
- Abantu bathi ngusukuma silingane ngoba liyanembuluka lisukume lomsuba nxa utsheba.

Phendula Le Imibuzo

Q: Qamba imhlobo emithathu yedelele.

Q: Kungani kuthiwa idelele ngusukuma silingane?

Q: Qamba okubili okufakwa edeleleni ukuze livuthwe kuhle libe buthakathaka.

Q: Kungani singambokothi idelele nxa lisanda kufakwe mbizeni.

Q: Xoxanini ngokunga nambithekisa idelele.

17 OKRA Continued

- Keep stirring after a short while and add a pinch of salt plus any other ingredients and seasoning you like to make it tastier and more appetising.
- After about 10 minutes, if you are satisfied that it is smooth and cooked enough, take off the pot and dish out.
- Okra is a very delicious traditional relish dish.
- People nickname it "*umaginyisa amathe*", saliva, meaning it makes you salivate, activates your appetite, "*inhliziyo ayibimnyama*".
- Okra is rich in vitamins and minerals and it boosts the body's immune system.
- People also nickname okra "*usukuma silingane*", 'stand up and let us see who will be taller'. This they say, describes the fact that it dribbles and hangs on following the ball of thick porridge, "*umsuba wesitshwala*" when you dip it in "*utsheba*" and lift it to your mouth.

Answer These Questions

Q: Name the three types of "idelele".

Q: Why is okra nicknamed 'one that says stand up let's see who is taller'?

Q: Name the two ingredients that are added to okra to make it cook soft.

Q: Why is the pot left open when one is cooking this dish?

Q: Name and discuss the ingredients added to okra in order to make it tastier.

18 UFUTHO

- Okudingekayo: imbiza, amanzi, lomumbu omanzi.
- Geca umumbu osesebuthakathaka.
- Uhlube wonke amakhasi ukhiphe lolevu lonke.
- Pheka umumbu lo unjalo useziqwini kumbe njalo uhululiwe.
- Uchaye wome endaweni ehlanzekileyo ubone ungawelinhlabathi inkobe zingalumela nxa usuwupheka kizo.
- Ebusika nxa usupheka inkobe zendumba, ezendlubu kumbe ezamazambane, thelekanisa lofutho lolo kuvuthwe ndawonye kubesakuthi yiwo amagwadla.
- Zinkobe ezimnandi ezakha lokuqinisa umzimba lezi. Kwakuthiwe esitwini zimnandi laloba kuphekelwa abakhwenyana umqhina inkobe ezilofutho.

Phendula Le Imibuzo

Q: Lwenziwa njani ufutho?

Q: Imibala yengcebethu yenziwa ngani?

Q: Ufutho lusetshenziswa kuphekwani?

Q: Ukhitshwa njani umumbu esiqwini?

Q: Ufutho enkobeni kuphekwa ngasiphi isikhathi somnyaka?

18 COOKED AND DRIED SOFT MAIZE

- Ingredients: water and maize kernels.
- Choose and cut the maize that is still soft, "*Umumbu omanzi/ obuthakathaka*".
- Remove all the husks, "*amakhasi*" and maize hair/silk, "*ulevu*"
- You can cook the maize either on the cob, "*ulesiqu*" or shelled, "*uhululiwe*".
- Spread it out on a clean surface away from sand and other debris like pebbles, preferably raised up from the floor.
- No one wants to chew "*inkobe*" with sand particles since "*ufutho*" is a vital ingredient of that dish.
- In winter or off-season, when you cook "*inkobe*", add "*ufutho*" instead of "*amagwadla*" to beans, peas, "*indumba*", roundnuts, "*indlubu*" or peanuts, "*amazambane*" as a way of varying the dishes.
- "*Ufutho*" makes "*inkobe*" dish even more tasty. This makes a filling and strengthening dish. The joke is that, with "*ufutho*", the dish is the best snack for even a son-in-law, it is, "*umqhina*".

Answer These Questions

Q: Discuss how one makes "*ufutho*".

Q: Discuss and describe how the colours on this vessel "*ingcebethu*" with "*ufutho*" are made.

Q: We use this ingredient when cooking which dish?

Q: What is the process of removing maize kernels from the cob called?

Q: During which season do we cook the dishes with "*ufutho*"?

19 IMIBHIDA

- Khana imibhida yakho yendumba, kumbe ibhobola lamathanga, eyolude loba eyesivandeni.
- Imibhida idliwa lesitshwala imanzi kumbe ichaywe yoma yabayimfushwa. Abanye bayadla imibhida lesinkwa kumbe lokunye ukudla abakuthamndayo.
- Uma usikha eyolude bathi ungayingcwebi ngozipho ngoba kuzakwengezelela ukubaba kwayo.
- Sikelela imibhida yakho nxa ingeyebhobola uqale uyihlube.
- Pheka imbhida emanzini amancinyane angaphansi kwayo.
- Phendula ufakisawudo.

19 LEAFY VEGETABLES

- Harvest the tender leaves of bean, pea or pumpkin vines, "*intanga/imilibo*" right towards their tips. Do the same if you are taking "*ulude*", "*imbuya*" or any other vegetables in the garden, "*esivandeni*".

- These vegetable dishes are traditionally eaten mainly with the staple dish of thick porridge, "*isitshwala*". They are eaten either fresh or dried and called "*umfushwa*".

- Some people like these vegetables with any other food or as fillings for snacks such as sandwiches.

- When harvesting, "*nxa usikha*", "*imbida yolude*" the "*ulude*" vegetable, it is said that you should not use your finger nails, "*inzipho*" to cut through it because it will taste more bitter, "*izababa kakhulu*".

- Wash, "*gezisa*", the vegetables thoroughly and then cut them finely. If cooking pumpkins, "*ibhobola*", remember to first peel off the spiky skin or fibre outside.

- Cook the vegetables in a little water but not so that it is drowning.

- Cover and let it cook for a few minutes.

- Open and turn the vegetables, adding enough salt to taste.

19 IMIBHIDA

(a) EYAMAFUTHA

- Emanzi, uma isivuthiwe, ikhiphe embizeni yonke.
- Tshiya imbiza ingelalutho ubusu thela amafutha wekele akhudumale angabili.
- Ungakhiphela imbiza, udiwo ngabe umphika phansi ukuze amafutha angeqi akutshise nxa usubisela imbhida.
- Bisela imbhida engelamsobho embizeni uphenduphendule ukhanzinge.
- Ungahle ufake lokunye okwengezelela ubunandi uhlanganisa labobilebile sakuthanda kwakho.
- Sibekela imbiza wekele ixhwathe kuvuthwe. Yephula imbiza uphakululele.

19 LEAFY VEGETABLES Continued

(a) USING COOKING OIL

- When cooked enough but still green, remove everything from the pot. Drain out the water if there is any left.
- Pour a little oil into the pot, not too much. Heat it up in a low heat.
- When oil, "*amafutha*" gets hot, "*esetshisa*", but not burning, "*engakabili*" take the pot down being careful "*unanzelele*" that no drop of water, "*amanzi*" comes into contact with the oil or the oil into spit and may catch on fire, "*umlilo*". That can cause a serious accident.
- Put the vegetables back into the pot or saucepan carefully, away from the fire or stove. While putting back the vegetables, be careful because any water dripping into the oil can pop up and burn your face or arms.
- Put the pot back on the heat and mix well, "*uphendu phendule*" frying, "*ukhanzinga*".
- At this point, you can add spices like chilli powder "*ibilebile*" and other types of seasoning.
- Cover the pot and let the food cook further keeping stirring it at short intervals.
- Dish up and serve after about ten minutes.

19 IMIBHIDA

(b) EYEDOBI

- Nxa isivuthiwe imbhida ikhiphe embizeni kusale umsobho wayo kuphela.
- Goqozela idobi esojeni ufake isawudo lokunye okunambithekisayo uma uthanda.
- Yekela kuxhwathe imizuzu engaba mine ubuphendula.
- Buyisela imibhida embizeni uhlanganise ledobi.
- Kwekele kuxhwathe eminye imizuzu engaba yisithupha ubuphendula emuva kwesikhatshana.
- Yephula imbiza uphakulule kudliwe.

(c) EYOLAZA

- Uma imbida isivuthiwe, cenga amanzi kumbe wekele atshe.
- Umlilo ubemlutshwana.
- Thela ulaza lwakho olwengule echagweni oluli hiqa.
- Phenduphendula ufake itshwayi lokunye okufunayo.
- Sibekela imbiza wekele kuxhwathe okungaba yimizuzu esitshiya galombili kodwa ubuphendula emva kwesikhatshana ukuze kungatsheli.
- Yephula imbiza uphakulule imuli idle.

19 LEAFY VEGETABLES Continued

(b) USING PEANUT BUTTER - "*IDOBI*"

- When the vegetables are satisfactorily cooked, one removes them from the pot leaving just the broth, "*umhluzi*".
- Add in and stir the peanut butter, smooth or the crunchy one. The amount depends on the amount of vegetables being cooked and your taste. Add a pinch of salt also to your taste.
- Cover and leave it to simmer for at least 4 minutes. Stir, checking the thickness of the "*isobho*". It should not be too watery "*amantshululu*".
- Put the vegetables back into the pot and mix them well with the simmering peanut butter gravy.
- Let the food cook for about 6 minutes but keep stirring about every 2 minutes during the process.
- The relish "*isitshebo*" can then be dished out and served so everyone enjoys this delicious meal.

(c) USING CREAM - "*ULAZA*"

- When well cooked, drain the water if there is any left.
- Make sure the heat is low otherwise the food will burn, "*ukutsha*" and smell, "*ukunuka*" in a way we call "*isihogolo*".
- Pour in the cream on top of the vegetables. The cream is traditionally the one removed "*ukwengula ulaza*" from seperating the milk "*ihiqa*".
- Mix well and add salt "*sawudo/itswayi/itshwayi*", to your taste.
- Some people add spices too at this stage.
- Place the lid back and leave to cook for about 8 minutes "*imizuzu etshiya ngalombili*". However, keep turning the food after about a minute or two to avoid the food burning, "*ukutshela*".
- Take down the pot and dish out. Serve the family and friends as relish for thick porridge, "*isitshwala*".

19 IMIBHIDA

Phendula Le Imibuzo

Q: Ngenjani imbida oyaziyo?

Q: Qamba imhlobo yemfushwa emithathu.

Q: Yiziphi indlela ezimbili zokupheki mbida?

Q: Lenziwani ibhobola lingaka sikelelwa?

Q: Imbida nxa siphekiwe isiyini?

19 LEAFY VEGETABLES Continued

Answer These Questions

Q: Which leafy vegetables do you know?

Q: Name three types of dried vegetables "imfushwa".

Q: Discuss any two methods of cooking these vegetables.

Q: Explain what is done to pumpkin leaves "ibhobola", before cutting them.

Q: What do we call the cooked dish of vegetables when it is ready?

20 UTSHWALA

- Okudingekayo: imithombo, impuphu, ugwaqo, imbiza, amaqhaga, ingqayi, isihluzo, inkezo/isiphungo, imbokodo, ingiga, umgigo, inkuni, amabele, uphoko, umumbu kumbe inyawuthi.
- Yenya ngokufaka emanzini amalutshwane imihlobo yamabele okhethe ukwenza ngayo imithombo ozayi sebenzisa.
- Sibekela ngesaka.
- Yekela kuthi fe ukumila.
- Khipha isaka wekele okolunyu suku.
- Khipha kumbe ngithi yenyula emanzini uchaye imithombo yome.
- Gwaqa ngempuphu mpuphu uyihlanganisa lamanzi abilayo.

20 TRADITIONAL BEER

- What is traditionally needed: fermentation flour "*imthombo*", *mealie* meal "*impuphu*", a stirring stick "*ugwaqo*", a drum or pot "*idramu/ifatshi kumbe imbiza*", clay vessels "*inqayi*", calabashes "*amaqhaga*", a sieve, "*isefa*", or the traditional woven strainer, "*isihluzo*", long handle gourds, "*inkezo/isiphungo*", grinding stones, "*ilitshe lembokodo*", flour receiving mat "*isithebe*", pounding vessel, "*ingiga*", pounding log, "*umgigo*", firewood, "*inkuni*", sorghum, "*amabele bele*", finger millet, "*uphoko*", maize or corn kernels, "*umumbu*" and pearl millet, "*inyawuthi*"

- Soak "*yenya*", the grains that will be used for boosting the fermentation process in some cold water.

- Cover with a sack "*isaka*" to both increase heat and keep it clean.

- Remove from the water and spread on a raised clean flat surface and cover when it is well soaked.

- Leave it until it germinates, "*ukumila*", to just short "*plumule*"/stems/shoots of the grain which should not grow too long.

- Remove the covering and leave for another day, "*ilanga/usuku*".

- Begin the process of making the beer by mixing maize meal and boiling water. This is called "*ukugwaqa*", or "*ukukhudumezela*" and is done in a drum by the fire.

- The mixture resulting from the process of "*ukugwaqa*", the name from the special stirring stick, "*ugwaqo*" is called "*inhlama*".

- Leave "*inhlama*" to cook like porridge.

- Remove and pour into two or three clean containers, this is to make smaller potions so that they may cool down quicker.

- When cold enough, such that by passing your clean hand through the mixture, you feel no heat at all, mix the portions in the bigger drum. Add the fermentation flour, about a 20 litre size bucketfuls, "*igokoko*" and mix well.

- The drum should be on or against a large fire. Usually outside or inside on the usual fireplace.

20 UTSHWALA

- Faka inhlama le ixhwathe ivuthwe eziko.
- Yephula uyekele kuphole.
- Hlanganisa lemithombo ubase umlilo wezigodo phandle uthele edilamini kumbe embizeni enkulu eseceleni komlilo lo.
- Thelamanzi kuhlambuluke ukuze kuxhwathe kubesalambazi elijiyileyo.
- Kungavuthwa sekungu mhiqo. Khipha kumbe yephula uyekele kuphole.
- Ungakha nje ngesiphungo inkezo yotshwala phela, unathe noma uthelele abantu emganwini badle umhiqo.
- Uma umhiqo usupholile waqanda mo, wuphose ke.
- Ukuphosa yikuhlanganisa umhiqo lemithombo oyomise wayichola ngembokodo elitsheni wayigiga engigeni ngomgigo yaba yimpuphu.
- Umakuyisikhathi somqando, ungafaka umquba ngaphansi kwembiza le loba ubase umlilo omlutshwana endlini le.
- Nqumisa ugwaqo phezu kwembiza wembese ngesaka.
- Isidudu butshwala obungakabilisisi.
- Nxa ugoqoza ubone sekugeleza ogwaqweni kuhitsha kumbe uthi uklwebhela umentshisi ucitshe, buzwakala buthi shwaa, bulegwebu elihle, sebubilile.

20 TRADITIONAL BEER Continued

- Pour water to make it like drinkable porridge not too watery though.
- Leave it to simmer and keep stirring with the "*ugwaqo*".
- When satisfactorily cooked, remove from the fire.
- This mixture is then called "*umhiqo*". Leave it to cool.
- People can scoop some out with "*inkezo/isiphungo*", the long handle gourd. Some may eat it from a bowl, "*umganu*" with spoons, "*izikhezo/izipunu*". It is a very popular drink with both the young and old.
- When "*umhiqo*" has cooled completely, add more fermentation flour "*imthombo*". This is called "*ukuphosa*". "*Imthombo*" can be of sorghum, finger millet or pearl millet.
- So, "*ukuphosa*", is to mix "*umhiqo*" with "*imthombo*" which germinated and was put out to dry before pounding or grinding it.
- If it is the cold season, in a more rurral setting, one may put some manure under the drum or keep a small fire burning in the room, "*indlu yotshwala*", to add heat.
- Place the beer stirring stick across the top of the drum or big clay pot to hold down the sack used as covering.
- When the fermentation process starts, the partly fermented beer "*obusese yisidudu*", is called "*obungaka bilisisi*".
- Full fermentation is checked by stirring and mixing the beer with "*ugwaqo*" then slowly lift the stick checking carefully. If it sticks to the stick, the drink is not ready yet. If however, it flows smoothly down the stick, and has a sharp smell that hits into your nose, "*ukuhitsha*", it is ready. The other way to check is to strike matches near the beer at the top of the drum. If it continues burning, then the beer is not ready yet. If on the other hand, the match fire quickly goes off, the beer is ready. The rattling sound of bubbles, "*shwaa shwaa shwa*" accompanied by a rising form of fluffy white froth, "*amagwebu*" these are key signs that this traditional beer has fully fermented. Not to forget the taste that should be sharp and bitter, not sweet, with a tightening feeling to the tongue.

20 UTSHWALA

- Ungabiza lezinye ingcitshi zikuzwele ukuze ungabu jujumezeli.
- Abanye babagoqozele imithombo emanzini ixwathiswe kube ngamasusu, bephule, bekele aphole amasusu, besebethela etshwaleni. Buphutshe ke igwebu buqhikile.
- Hluzela enkonxeni ngokukha embizeni ngesiphungo, inkezo yotshwala uthela esefeni elezikhala ezingcinyane kumbe esihluzweni eselukwe ngemizi.
- Ukuhluza yikwehlukanisa insipho lotshwala. Thela utshwala osebuhluziwe enqayini kumbe emaqhageni.
- Nxusa izihlobo labomakhelwana abanathayo, bazonatha.
- Uma ubuqondile buyimbamba sibili, uzwa sebetshotshi ngoma begida lengxoxo isithe mbo. Isiyiwowowo sekusengwa lezimithiyo ke lapho.
- Utshwala obunathwa kuphendukwa kusisa, libhabhalazi.
- Ngosuku lwesithathu buyabe sebutshodile ngakho buyavuselelwa ngamasusu sebusiba ngobamangqindi.

20 TRADITIONAL BEER Continued

- One can invite other knowledgeable traditional beer brewers, "*ingcitshi*", or even a drinker known to know the difference well, to advise you. All these are efforts to try and avoid a premature or unsatisfactory finish, "*ukubujujumezela*", after so much work.

- Sometimes traditional beer brewers add "*amasusu*" to strengthen the fermentation before making final checks. "*Amasusu*" are quickly cooked using a mixture of left over "*imthombo*" and cold water. One stirs and leaves to cook or simmer for about 10 minutes. Leave the misture to cool and add to the drum of beer. The fermentation will intensify, the sound and bubbles making froth and foam also increasing "*buphutshe*", letting off steam.

- Using "*isiphungo*", scoop the beer out of the drum and pour it through the sieve or the traditional "*isihluzo*" made of "*imizi*", grass mat and "*ilala or uswenyane*". Have a clean bucket underneath the strainer so that the strained beer flows through into it. Empty the residue, "*insipho*" that is left in the strainer into another clean container.

- Pour "*thela*", the beer into clay pots, "*inqayi*" and calabashes, "*amaqhaga*" ready to be served out.

- Invite relatives, friends and neighbours to come to drink and enjoy, if they drink that is?

- Some people just know the process of brewing traditional beer even though they themselves do not drink it.

- If you have got it right, "*ubuqondile*", it is what is called "*imbamba yomqombothi*". You will hear people starting to sing all kinds of songs "*betshotsha ingoma*", dancing "*begida*" and many discussions, "*ingxoxo*" getting louder and many, with a lie or two thrown in to exaggerate arguments for some. For those "*labo*", there is a saying "*kuthiwa sebesenga lezimithiyo*", they are said to be enjoying the beer so much, they are now milking even those in gestation.

20 UTSHWALA

- Ngolwesine usuku sekunga xhwathiswa insipho zithelwe lamasusu lazo zivuselelwe.
- Lo sungumtshayiwa ivanya phela.
- Utshwala bungaba ngobomsebenzi njengobe lima lemithethelo, kumbe obomdlalo wokuzithokozisa. Obunye bungaba ngobemali obokuthengisa.
- Utshwala bulengcitshi, yikho abanye babacele kumbe babhadale zona zibasize, hawu zibuqonde, banathe bahambe sebedakwe sebekhuluma bodwa bedayizela beqhubimbuzi ezingekho.

20 TRADITIONAL BEER Continued

- When people come back on the second day for beer, any leftovers "*ibhabhalazi*", they may have a hangover.

- On the third day, if any is left, it no longer tastes very good. They say "*sebutshodile*", it has lost its vibe. To revive it "*ukubuvuselela*", "*amasusu*" are cooked as discussed above, left to cool and then poured into that beer which, after straining out, "*insipho*", with the sieve, is now called "*obamanqindi*".

- On the forth day, there is no more beer left but because it was so nice, some people will still come to check. The brewer will then mix all the beer residue, "*insipho*", "*zonke*", and cook them mixed with some more of "*amasusu*", to revive it further.

- This type of beer is then called "*umtshayiwa*" and also "*ivanya*".

- The beer can be for "*ilima*" when friends and neighbours are asked to come and help with some work, "*umsebenzi*". It can also be brewed for cultural ceremonies or for birthday celebrations and even to sell, "*oboku thengisa*".

- Traditional beer brewing has specialists, that is why some people ask or pay for those who have such experience to come and help them, "*zibasize*". When they get it all just right, some people walk about from side to side, "*bedayizela*", of the path talking to themselves "*bekhuluma bodwa*". The joke said is that, they are walking like someone herding non-existent goats "*ukuqhuba imbuzi ezingekho*"!

20 UTSHWALA

Phendula Le Imibuzo

Q: Insipho zikhitshwa ngani etshwaleni?

Q: Utshwala nxa sebuqhiliki gwebu sebunjani?

Q: Buthelwa ngaphi osebu hluziwe?

Q: Osedakwe kakhulu bathi uhambe qhubani?

Q: Inkezo yotshwala kuthiwa yini?

Q: Utshwala obutshodileyo obuvuselelwe ngamasusu kuthiwa ngoba?

Q: Ababuyela etshwaleni ngakusisa bayanatha Obani?

Q: Nxa sebuphelile utshwala ngosuku lwesine kuxhwathiswa insipho sebubizwa kuthiwe yini?

Q: Oqalisa utshwala sithi wenzani?

Q: Qamba okuthathu okunga phekelwa utshwala.

20 TRADITIONAL BEER *Continued*

Answer These Questions

Q: What is used to separate beer and "insipho"?

Q: When the beer is foaming and frothy we say it is what?

Q: Discuss how and where clean strained beer is poured before it is served.

Q: What is someone very drunk said to be doing on the way home?

Q: Name the traditional gourd used like a cup.

Q: What is the name given to the last of the actual beer that is revived with "amasusu"?

Q: Those going back to drink beer on the day after, are going for which one? Discuss.

Q: Explain what is done on the fifth day and name the beer people drink on that day.

Q: What are the terms used to describe the first process of actually cooking the beer?

Q: Discuss three things or occasions for which traditional beer can be brewed.

IZIMPENDULO

OMAMA ABAGIGAYO / THE POUNDING MOTHERS

Q1 i. Yimthombo / Fermented and germinated grain flour
ii. Ngamatshakada / Samp / Skinless maize kernels
iii. Iidobi / Peanut butter
iv. Iswayi / Imhwabha egigiweyo / Pounded dry meat
v. Ngamabele / Any grain like sorghum / Amabelebele, Fingermillet / Uphoko or pearlmillet / inyawuthi

Q2 Ingiga lo mgigo / Pounding vessel and pounding pole.

TOPIC 01 - AMATSHAKADA kumbe UMNGUTSHU

Q1 Uthela amanzi akhudumalayo, atshisayo loba abilayo / Pour warm, hot or boiling water.

Q2 Ngamazambane / Peanuts, Indlubu / Roundnunts, Indumba / Peas / Beans, Peanutbutter / Idobi or cream / Ulaza.

Q3 When eaten with meat, it is called Umngqutshu.

TOPIC 02 - UMXHANXA

Q1 Umumbu owomileyo/dry kernels or amagwadla, Ijodo / Melon and water / Amanzi.

Q2 Sihlanyela intanga / We sow a seed.

Q3 Ijodo elonyisiweyo / A dried melon.

TOPIC 03 - ILAMBAZI / IYAMBAZI / PORRIDGE

Q1 a. Ekuseni / At breakfast time.
b. Ogulayo kumbe o beletheyo / For a sick person or for one who has just given birth or misscarried.
c. Usane / Ingane / A baby.

Q2 The porridge for babies is called ingcumbe, yet porridge for a sick person, is called Umphungo.

Q3 Sour porridge is called elibilisiweyo / Fermented one.

ANSWERS

TOPIC 04 - UMUMBU OMANZI / FRESH SOFT MAIZE

Q1   Ungamachaphazi.

Q2   Umtsheketshela / Tassels.

Q3   Uwosiwe / Roasted or grilled, Boiled / Uphekiwe, uyizinkwa zomfahlwa / Ground and made into dumpling like balls wrapped in husks before cooking.

FUN ACTIVITY

Sing the song that some adults sing as they shell and eat kernels from a child's cob of fresh roast or cooked maize saying they are helping to start the path or way. You can do it as individuals, pairs or groups. Discuss the songs origin.

TOPIC 05 - INOPI kumbe ISIJEZA / Melon with Mealie Meal

Q1   Yintanga / Vine.

Q2   Lunkankalu / Dried melon.

Q3   Ijodo lempuphu loba amanzi / Melon and grain flour or water .

TOPIC 06 - AMAGWADLA / BOILED DRY KERNELS

Q1   Ngamaputi.

Q2   Ngumphako / Snack.

Q3   Owomileyo / Dry maize kernels.

TOPIC 07 - ISITSHWALA / THICK PORRIDGE

Q1   Siyaphehla / We beat with a beater.

Q2   Ngophini / The stirring stick.

Q3   Ngumsuba / Thick porridge ball we dip into relish and eat.

Q4   Lesitshebo / Relish.

IZIMPENDULO

TOPIC 08 - AMAHEWU / GRAIN FLOUR DRINK

Q1 Yimthombo le fulawa / Fermented and germinated grain flour and plain flour.

Q2 When people are invited for work which is called ilima.

Q3 Isitshwala kumbe ilambazi / Thick porridge or just porridge

Q4 Ayanathwa / One drinks amahewu.

TOPIC 09 - AMAQEBELENGWANE / GRAIN FLOUR DUMPLINGS

Q1 Akhudumalayo / Warm water.

Q2 Unatha okuthile / With a drink.

TOPIC 10 - INKOBE / LEGUME and KERNELS DISH

Q1 Ezendlubu / Roundnuts, Ezamazambane / Peanuts, Ezendumba / Peas or Beans.

Q2 Ufutho / Fresh maize kernels boiled then dried to recook with legumes in off-season.

Q3 Unathe okutshisayo uzidla / Have a hot drink as you eat.

Q4 Ezila matshe / Ones with sand particles.

TOPIC 11 - AMAKHOWA / MUSHROOMS

Q1 Awesiduli / Hill ones, Indlebe kagogo / Grandma's ear, Indevu zika babamkhulu / Granddad's beard or any other three.

Q2 Inkowankowane / The ones called inkowane.

Q3 Uyakukha / Going to fetch.

TOPIC 12 - IDOBI / PEANUT BUTTER

Q1 Siyacacada / We are shelling.

Q2 Yikuqunta / Pulling peanut pods off the plant.

Q3 Ngembokodo le litshe / Special stones big one Ilitshe smaller one Imbokodo.

ANSWERS

TOPIC 13 - AMACIMBI / AMAPHANE WORMS

Q1 Ugola amacimbi / We say "*uyagola*".

Q2 Liphane / It is the phane tree.

Q3 Ngamavevane / Butterflies.

Q4 Ngameva ayahlaba / Their spikes are pricky and / Njalo Ayangcolisa okungaphumiyo esigqokweni / They badly stain clothes too.

Activity

Imitate / Lingiselanini ukuhamba kwecimbi / the movement of icimbi with your finger alone or as groups.

TOPIC 14 - AMATHANGA LAMAKHOMANE / PUMPKINS AND FRESH TENDER GOURDS

Q1 Ithanga eselikhule laqedela likhulu kulekhomane esiliphekayo / The ripe pumpkin is bigger than the tender gourd that we cook.

Q2 Zingcezu / Pieces.

Q3 It is called eseli kombile / The dry one.

Q4 Yintanga / A vine.

Q5 Ngezitsha / The special vessels called 'isitsha'- (singular), 'izitsha'- (plural) usually made of ilala fibres and umhlomelelo womadodlwane the broom grass.

TOPIC 15 - ISAHLAKA ISATHUBI LESATHIYANE / THE COLOSTRUM AND WHOLE MILK / DAIRY DISHES

Q1 Isahlaka / Colostrum only dish.

Q2 Ngomama lamankazana / Amantombazana / Women and girls.

Q3 Ngezibayeni / By the corrals / Cowsheds.

Q4 Kusukela kuqeda ukusengelwa isahlaka lize libeliguqa liphuse / From end of colostrum dish cooking to the time the calf is weaned.

Q5 The cow udder cracks and gets sore causing pain and anger to the cow. That starves the calf and deprives people of milk.

IZIMPENDULO

TOPIC 16 - UMCABA / CURDS AND SORGHUM FLOUR DISH

Q1 Luhayezi / It is called uhayezi.

Q2 Yikuphothula / Preparing the dish is called ukuphothula umcaba.

Q3 Red Swazi, iTsweta, iSibhuku, Lundende and Rada.

Q4 The curds calabash is called igula.

Q5 Umunge that is at the bottom of igula which lets out whey, is closed with ingcotho. A small clean piece of material especially pure cotton, can be tightly twisted and used as a stopper too.

Q6 Babekhangezwa bemukele zandla zombili bakhothe / They received with both hands and licked.

TOPIC 17 - IDELELE / OKRA

Q1 Elemasimini umdlothi / The fields one called umdlothi, Elezidaka / Wild one from muddy arears, and the exotic one with seeds / Elentanga.

Q2 It dribbles following the hand and the lump of isitshwala / umsuba, that we dip into it / Liyagxoza lisukuma lilandela as if to match our height, if we dared to stand up to the challenge.

Q3 Bicarbonate Soda and Ashes.

Q4 Liyaluluma liphuphume / It bubbles and overflows.

Q5 Spices, tomatoes, chilli etc.

TOPIC 18 - UFUTHO / COOKED FRESH MAIZE KERNELS DRIED

Q1 Pheka inhlamvu zomumbu omanzi uzichaye endaweni ehlanzekileyo ephakemeyo zome / Cook the shelled fresh soft maize kernels and dry them covered lightly on a clean raised surface to prevent sand and other debris.

Q2 For the colour / Umphendulo like one on this ingcebethu fibres, traditionally people use known tree roots / Impande, tree bark / Amaxolo or leaves / Amahlamvu.

Q3 Inkobe / Legume and maize kernel dishes.

ANSWERS

Q4   Uyahululwa / It is shelled.

Q5   Ebusika / During the off season .

TOPIC 19 - IMBIDA / LEAFY VEGETABLES

Q1   Eyendumba / Peas and Beans one, Eyebhobola / Pumpkin one, Eyolude / The slightly bitter one, Eyembuya / African spinach one and the exotic ones like Cabbage.

Q2   Umfushwa wendumba / Dried Peas or Beans vine leaves one, Umfushwa wolude / Dried bitter one and Umfushwa webhobola / Dried tender Pumpkin leaves one.

Q3   Adding oil / Amafutha, adding Idobi / Peanut butter and Ulaza / Cream.

Q4   Liyahlutshwa intanjana ezihlabayo / Peel off the spiky fibres.

Q5   Yisitshebo / It is relish.

TOPIC 20 - UTSHWALA / TRADITIONAL BEER

Q1   Ngesefa / Sieve or Ngesihluzo / Traditional Strainer.

Q2   Sebubilile / It has fully fermented.

Q3   Emaqhageni le ngqayini / In calabashes and traditional clay pots.

Q4   Goats / Imbuzi.

Q5   Yi siphungo / The dry long-handled gourd or wooden long-handled one.

Q6   Ngobamangqindi.

Q7   Obebhabhalazi.

Q8   Yivanya / Ngǔmtshayiwa.

Q9   Uyagwaqa / Uyagudumezela.

Q10   Ngumthethelo / The traditional ceremony for appeasing ancestors, ngobe lima / For people invited for work, Kumbe obomdlalo loba uyiwuphi nje / And for any other celebrations and get-togethers.

Printed in Great Britain
by Amazon